T3-BNG-802

MGEN
NE948

Magic

& Hypersystems

Constructing the Information-Sharing Library

HAROLD BILLINGS

AMERICAN LIBRARY ASSOCIATION
Chicago
2002

h28428274

While extensive effort has gone into ensuring the reliability of information appearing in this book, the publisher makes no warranty, express or implied, on the accuracy or reliability of the information, and does not assume and hereby disclaims any liability to any person for any loss or damage caused by errors or omissions in this publication.

Portions of this book have been previously published—several in somewhat different versions—in the following journals: "Libraries, Language, and Change: Defining the Information Present" in *College & Research Libraries;* "Shared Collection Building: Constructing the Twenty-First-Century Relational Research Library" and "Library Collections and Distance Information: New Models of Collection Development for the Twenty-First Century" in *Journal of Library Administration;* "Governing Library Networks: The Quick and the Dead for the 1990s," "Magic and Hypersystems: A New Orderliness for Libraries," and "The Bionic Library" in *Library Journal;* "Supping with the Devil: New Library Alliances in the Information Age," "The Information Ark: Selection Issues in the Preservation Process," and "The Tomorrow Librarian" in *Wilson Library Bulletin;* and "Special Collections: Still Special after All These Years" in *RBM: Rare Books, Manuscripts, and Cultural Archives.* "Magic and Hypersystems" was also included in *Library Lit. 21—The Best of 1990.* "Giving Up Prophecy: The Future of Information Cooperation" owes some of its text to "TexShare and GALILEO: Comments on Managed Information Sharing," published in *Texas Library Journal.* Used with permission of the Texas Library Association.

The paper used in this publication meets the minimum requirements of American National Standard for Information Sciences—Permanence of Paper for Printed Library Materials, ANSI Z39.48-1992. ∞

Library of Congress Cataloging-in-Publication Data

Billings, Harold, 1931-
 Magic and hypersystems : constructing the information-sharing library / by Harold Billings.
  p. cm.
 ISBN 0-8389-0834-9 (alk. paper)
  1. Library science—Technological innovations. 2. Library information networks. 3. Library cooperation. 4. Information technology. 5. Collection development (Libraries). 6. Research libraries—Automation. I. Title.
 Z678.9 .B55 2002
 021.6'5—dc21   2002005338

Copyright © 2002 by the American Library Association. All rights reserved except those which may be granted by Sections 107 and 108 of the Copyright Revision Act of 1976.

Printed in the United States of America.

06 05 04 03 02   5 4 3 2 1

To My Family

With grateful appreciation to Francis Miksa,
extraordinary scholar and teacher,
and
GraceAnne Andreassi DeCandido,
a superlative editor, librarian, and friend,
for their inspiration and assistance

CONTENTS

PREFACE

During the initial years of what we now might recognize as the front edge of the electronic information revolution, and throughout its subsequent unfolding, I had the good fortune to be directly involved in both national library resource-sharing efforts and the local construction of new programs and services to take advantage of the opportunities then surfacing. Service on the boards of several major library organizations helped provide me with additional perspectives on the management of centralized support systems for distributed library memberships. Discussion and debate with leaders in the profession, and with thoughtful colleagues at home, were invaluable. The administration of a huge research library was an instructive counterpoint. The hours spent exploring the commercial Internet and applying Web-based advantages to the creation of an institutional online library also have been informative, inspirational, and entertaining. What have I not touched! What has not touched me?

These experiences led in time to an interest in sharing my personal observations about this refulgent period in contemporary library history. Thinking and writing about my experiences provided an opportunity to compare typical library tasks within the context of both physical and digital environments. It also offered the opportunity to look ahead and suggest the nudging of some of those activities in directions not necessarily under consideration. Weak oracular, strong skeptical genes must be a part of my makeup.

These observations have made it apparent that librarianship stands before a remarkable opportunity. A great twenty-first-century relational library sprawls ready for further construction and refinement. I have been fortunate to witness the foundational steps of this Promethean achievement, and am grateful to ponder these circumstances and write about them both as they occurred and in present contemplation. And here is the result, a contemporary record of the revolution as it touched various library activities, with ripples of change spreading throughout the means by which libraries have organized knowledge, and a description of the permuting relational library system from a new century's point of view. The present achievement in libraries and learning is surely a small miracle in comparison with what is to come.

I am greatly indebted to those colleagues who afforded me the opportunity to participate in the organizations, the conversations, and the field-work that underlie this work, and who have been patient with my musings and grumbling discourses on these issues over the years. There is no adequate means to thank those many library staff members at the University of Texas, nearly fifty years of them, who helped awaken this once-sleeping library, and me.

1

Libraries and
Other Networked Botanies

The last decade of the twentieth century, and the initial years of the twenty-first, have seen the most dramatic changes in libraries in their many centuries of evolution. While political walls have fallen, statues tumbled, the currencies of great nations given up for a common new unit, and the globe has been enwrapped in an electronic web, libraries too have been subjected to economic, social, technological, and other transformative forces that have brought constant, consuming change.

The information revolution especially, in a few quick years, has engulfed libraries as it has most of the world. Its forces have been dominant, quick, and overwhelming; they continue to touch and transform virtually every task and service in librarianship. The issues they raise are just beginning to be sorted out. Progress has indeed been made in meeting the challenge and grasping its opportunity, but has been slowed somewhat by the fact that libraries, and the educational community of which they are a part, have not entirely learned how to make use of recent developments in telecommunications and information technology.

Reflections on culture and the human and natural record precede discovery and knowledge. The transmitted human record—oral, graphic, print, sound, emotive, electronic—passing from one generation to another, from a scholar to a learner, of content to a reader or listener or viewer, underlies these considerations. Libraries are the traditionally accepted collectors, custodians, and managers of these records—the printed and recorded word, artifacts and the natural record, physical or digital. Libraries are the primary contributors to the preservation and transmittal of culture, history, science, and our earth's record in any format to the learning fields of knowledge.

Libraries have profited from the new technologies in pursuing these historic responsibilities, but the full challenge and fresh possibilities offered by these tools lie beyond an uncertain horizon. It took many permutations of the lever, the fulcrum, and the wheel to enable Gutenberg's machine. Like the device that sent a flood of words into other information streams and organizational models, the technologies of today offer a means for information seekers and learners to extend their explorations to both physical and digital collections—to a vast emerging global information commons—without restrictions of time, or place, or purpose.

What are the major barriers to more fully enable this reach to the informational and learning stars? Economic impediments, the inertia of ponderous social institutions, and a general distaste for change represent the major obstacles. Like other institutions beset by uncertainties, libraries tend to seek solutions in the models to which they are most accustomed—to pursue whatever flag carries the colors they have known, while ignoring, overlooking, or fearing signage pointing to an unknown or unexpected success. Transformation has been met with the use of both old responses and new ones, with old tools and newly created ones, the usefulness of which is still to be determined.

Relationships among the knowledge agents in this new age are especially uncertain, and, in some cases, troubling. I fear that too much of the library community is becoming estranged from the publishing industry and information market with whom libraries must collaborate. Each player on the knowledge scene must retain an appropriate balance of responsibility and reward in the complex information flow. Trust is important. There is too much uninformed, ill-advised, and precipitous rebellion against the traditional publishing establishment.

Librarians have never driven the publishing enterprise. They have selected, organized, and provided access to its results. Technology is altering methodologies, but not the basic roles of the many important players in scholarly communication and the general publishing process. Relationships among libraries are also changing, and new cooperative organizational models (chiefly consortia seeking to extend their financial resources) are achieving varying degrees of effectiveness. Some older organizations continue with fresh purpose and renewed success—although librarians still cling to others that perhaps should have been let adrift long ago.

This cycle of essays and papers has developed from the foregoing considerations. To some degree, this volume is a biography of the transformed research library as it stands at a moment in time—a time defined by the most recent of these writings—and how it arrived there. This book begins with historical comparisons of the similarities of contemporary information systems with sixteenth-century attempts to order knowledge based on "magic" image-based memory systems—the seminal origins of the Web. Various essays then examine the foundational politics and changing nature of contemporary library organizations; the state of partnering in the information flow; the future of library education and librarianship; the critical nature of selection in the preservation process; new models of shared collection building, information access, and associated economic trends; the changing language of librarianship and how it helps define the present situation— all leading up to the dynamic building and binding of both physical and digital libraries, as embodied in a twenty-first-century relational library model being constructed around us in a global information commons.

By reviewing the historical foundations of this new model through a single critical eye, an attempt is made to determine how libraries can better understand and use these transformative forces to shape a stronger information world. It is evident that neither the issues nor the ideas presented here have grown stale during this transformative period, nor is it likely that this situation will stabilize in the near future. Observing this situation in fresh ways may help librarians understand how they can deal with problems in the future, within the daily constants of library operations and services, despite changes in the historical staging around them. Or, contrarily, how changes in the social, fiscal, technological, or learning landscape may affect library operations, programs, and services beyond the immediate horizon.

Thus, a consideration of the historical record, a representation of today's changing library and information world, and the application of new ideas may identify the foundations of these changes and signal more clearly where libraries, information management, and knowledge systems now stand and where they are bound.

Several chapters of this book have purposely been left marked with the signs of their day. Like photographs of old libraries with automobiles or persons in strange attire around them that reveal the earlier date of the pictures, we note that the buildings and their services are just as germane to users now as they were then. This approach and its textual style attempt to draw on the richness of human history and culture to relate specific library issues to earlier traditions, as well as to the contemporary society that librarians serve. Despite the many changes in the means by which information has been recorded, preserved, and transmitted to contemporary users, there continues an enduring thread of values and worth over many centuries for what we know as librarianship. It is sometimes only made apparent by a word, a symbol, a sign left from the past, that these roots continue today as they once did, as they will into the future despite ongoing capitulations to change.

This connection of libraries past, libraries present, libraries future is emblematic of the small separations in time of knowledge and humankind from their forebears, the brief mileage between centuries, the ongoing long passage of words and ideas and human values in the few days given the messengers to pass those batons to runners ahead. The architect Charles Eames—a genius at integrating imagery and ideas from a diversity of sources into new works of art, architecture, and design in the mid-twentieth century—has said of constructing the *object* what could just as well be said of that greater gift that libraries offer for constructing new knowledge and imagination from sources scattered throughout their physical and digital shelves: "The connections, the connections. It will in the end be these details that . . . give the product its life."[1]

Knowledge might just as well be the "product" that Eames describes as are art and design. Ralph Caplan explains of Eames's comment: "Connections between what? Between such disparate materials as wood and steel, between such seemingly alien disciplines as physics and painting, between clowns and mathematical concepts, between people—architects and mathematicians and poets and philosophers and corporate executives. . ."[2] Similarly, it is out of varied gleanings from books and other sources in library collections that scholars are able to build a renascent learning and knowledge structure, connecting minds and tools for action.

Librarianship at its best is a Renaissance enterprise. Evidence of the linkage of our days with that explosion of learning is a precious thing. It could be instructive for librarians to remember, for example, that the word "network," as we recognize it, was first used by Sir Thomas Browne in *The Garden of Cyrus* (1658) to describe the living order of nature—libraries being, I am convinced, just as elegantly alive and susceptible to how we tend them today as were the botanies in Sir Thomas's Garden.

> Now although this elegant ordination of vegetables, hath found coincidence or imitation in sundry works of Art, yet is it not also destitute of naturall examples, and though overlooked by all, was elegantly observable, in severall works of nature. . . . The same is observably effected in . . . pendulous excrescencies of severall Trees, of Wallnuts, Alders, and Hazels, which hanging all the Winter, and maintaining their Net-worke close, by the expansion thereof are the early foretellers of the Spring.

The essays in this book may suggest, at times, a repeal of orthodoxy and the received mind-set of the profession. They were meant to. Librarians must be willing to take fresh looks at old things, to try new ones, must be willing to build new structures that might better support the mission of libraries to freshen learning and knowledge, and be just as willing to give up what does not work. Any one of these—the look, the try, the building, the tearing down—may be the hardest to implement.

A willingness to change is what the quickening of knowledge is all about. Perhaps the issues and ideas considered in these texts will encourage the efforts required to advance libraries more creatively through the ongoing information revolution, to gain good heart, to look for new tricks up knowledge's sleeves in a coming spring.

NOTES

1. *Connections: The Work of Charles and Ray Eames,* with an essay by Ralph Caplan. Catalog of an exhibition at the Frederick S. Wight Art Gallery, University of California, Los Angeles, December 1976–February 1977 (Los Angeles: UCLA Art Council, 1976), 48.
2. Ibid.

2

~~~

Magic and Hypersystems
A New Orderliness for Libraries

The knowledge situation of the late sixteenth century was much like the present. That era was also flooded with new information formats, a rapid expansion of knowledge, and efforts to order knowledge through systems that extended the capabilities of the mind. There was a breaching of previously accepted boundaries of place and time through the introduction of a thought model that accepted and transcended Copernicanism. A comparison of our time with the historical foundations of memory and knowledge systems astir in the sixteenth century offers insights into the present situation and suggests where our knowledge systems are bound.

The Growth of Knowledge

For all the wider sowing of knowledge afforded by the printing press, perhaps its greatest contribution lay in its secularization of knowledge. The place of books in those days was little in the academies and universities of the time, but much within the church. Thought imprisoned by either the Inquisition or the Reformation was dead seed, but printing helped revive it. Dogma was replaced with new intellectual opportunities, and the revolutions in thought that followed should not have been surprising. It is certainly not surprising that reactionary

---

This article was originally published in *Library Journal* 115 (April 1, 1990).

agencies of both church and court found an intensely magnified challenge as the printed word and an astonishing new inquisitiveness awakened throughout the intellectual world.

How to organize this flush of books and ideas must have represented a real problem to those institutions and individuals that soon found themselves swamped with printed items. Print had to take its place among the manuscripts of the day, and this added considerably to the space required for storage. The *armarium,* or book chest, was no longer sufficient to hold the library of the time; and an unaided mind or memory was seen as inadequate for all the learning and lore set loose in the world.

Memory Arts in Ordering Knowledge

For centuries, the art of memory had served as a major means for transmitting oral tradition and had played a significant part in the art of rhetoric. From the days of the poet Simonides (5th century BC), who, as told by Cicero, introduced the classical art of memory, the memory arts had helped organize knowledge and carry it forward. Memory arts were a major intellectual tool utilized for nineteen light and dark centuries before the Renaissance. It can easily be understood how the memory arts—if generally regarded by the sixteenth century as a medieval scheme and no longer necessary for carrying the word into the future—nevertheless would early be looked to for help in organizing the storehouses of knowledge that grew so soon from Gutenberg's machine.[1]

The human mind was seen as the device within which the memory arts could organize and relate the knowledge of the times.

Classical mnemonics held as a major principle the role of place and image in vitalizing the imagination of the ancient rhetor to recall his text. Simonides was said to have identified for relatives the mangled dead in the ruins of a devastated banquet hall by recollecting where diners had been seated. Thus, in the classical mnemonic, an elaborate building was visually imprinted on the mind, with all its features and furnishings to be recalled turn by turn, so that images in a text could be associated with scenes, and image and embedded text could be recollected as each feature of the building was revisited in the memory.

A theater or its stage, called to the mind's eye, became common to this classical architectural mnemonic. By the 1530s (when appreciation for the classical arts had revived), Giulio Camillo of Venice achieved fame for constructing a wooden theater filled with images and boxes, ordered and graded, to function as an elaborate memory system. Several centuries earlier, Ramon Lull laid the foundations for future memory systems by devising an "art" to relate the encyclopedia of knowledge by revolving wheels of divine attributes.

In the late sixteenth century, Giordano Bruno devised several magic memory systems (conceived on "magical" rather than natural images) that, while very much based on the ancient precepts of place and image, located astral images on a revolving Lullian wheel. There, virtually "every possible arrangement and combination of objects in the lower world—plants, animals, stones—would be perceived and remembered" by their relationship through innumerable metaphysical layers with a mystical, higher Unity.

Fifty years later, in the early seventeenth century, Robert Fludd would maintain these common threads by devising a theatre memory system that combined a visualization of the stages of "real" public theaters with astrological images.

A wonderful genealogical memory tree could be constructed leading from Simonides through these increasingly magical thinkers of the Renaissance to the eventual spilling out of new "methods" of modern science—still linked to magical memory systems—from the minds of Bacon, Descartes, and Leibniz in the seventeenth century.

Under a variety of other codes—concepts of magic seals, astral images, emblems, colors, pictures, mathematical characters, objects, signs, symbols, sigils—the visualization of images and places was incorporated into numerous other efforts at developing memory systems. These attempted to relate and organize the extant universe of knowledge within the human mind—for the retrieval of information, for the discovery of new knowledge, and for bringing the individual closer to the divine.

Dame Frances Yates (1899–1981) was a pioneer historian of the memory arts and did much to relate that topic to the flowering of modern science, though it passed through dark and magical places in doing so. By the sixteenth century, she writes, "The printed book is destroying age-old memory habits," but adds, "Nevertheless, far from waning, the art of memory had actually entered upon a new and strange lease of life . . . . Through Renaissance Neoplatonism, with its Hermetic core, the art of memory was once more transformed, this time into a Hermetic or occult art."[2]

Occultism was just as much a part of the learned scene as superstition and magic were part of the woof of all human existence. John Crowley, in an illuminating work on ghosts in Shakespeare, has described a body of common wisdom regarding the supernatural that "extended through all strata of society."[3] "It should not be forgotten," Crowley says, "that Elizabethan nights were darker than ours, roads longer, Hell nearer. The natural world had not yet divided itself from man's moral apprehension." Yates characterized the times as a "Renaissance borderland country, half magic, half emerging science." In the spindrift of ideas thrown off by the Renaissance, real science was never far from pseudoscience, or the two were so commingled that it was difficult to distinguish them. Astronomy, mathematics, and geometry were not far removed from alchemy, astrology, geomancy, and hermetism.

Libraries were gradually drawn into this maelstrom of new ideas and a world of knowledge in turmoil. In the 1550s during the English Reformation, there was a great plunder and dissolution of the cloisters, and the monastery libraries that had guarded what little there was of the written heart of learning for a thousand dark years were almost completely scattered. At particular risk were any works that appeared "popish." Books or manuscripts containing mathematical diagrams were regarded with particular suspicion. It has been estimated that only 2 percent of the 300,000 volumes in over 800 monastery libraries survived the review of reformers.[4]

Dee and Bruno

Yates not only established the concept of the importance of hermetical influences on the development of modern science, but also laid the major responsibility for this movement on two magus philosophers, John Dee (1527–1608) and Giordano Bruno (1548–1600).

John Dee—astronomer, mathematician, toolmaker, magus, and librarian—suggested to Queen Mary as early as 1556 that the dispersed monastic collections be regathered to form a great national library, but nothing came of the notion. Dee then began the building of a personal library that by 1583 numbered over 4,000 books and manuscripts—perhaps the largest library in England, and certainly the greatest accumulation of scientific information at that time. By contrast, the library of Sir Thomas Bodley, when he retired in 1587 to "set up his Staffe at the Librarie dore in Oxon," numbered only 2,000 volumes.

After casual dismissal as a quirky, minor player on the Elizabethan intellectual scene prior to Yates's studies, Dee has been credited more recently with being at the very center of an academy of learning in England in the last quarter of the sixteenth century. Elizabeth, Sir Philip Sidney, and a circle of literary and scientific friends are known to have spent time at Mortlake, Dee's home. But Dee's interest in mathematics, mechanics, and magic was not in the mainstream of the emerging humanist movement, but rather an occult and even dangerous interest that could be pursued in the countryside, but not at court.

Nevertheless, Dee was an adviser to Elizabethan mariners, worked on scientific instruments, shared his foreign-gained knowledge of geography in advancing navigation, and is credited with spreading a knowledge of Copernican astronomy among English scientists. He composed a preface to the English translation of the works of Euclid that, according to Frances Yates, "As a manifesto for the advancement of science . . . is of greater importance than Francis Bacon's."[5] At the same time, he composed a description of his attempts to conjure angels through cabalistic numerology. He reputedly constructed a mechanical stage machine, a flying scarabaeus that carried a man and a basket of "victuales" to the top of Trinity Hall, Cambridge. These widely disparate exercises of intellect and ingenuity, while perhaps the most marked signs of a universal Renaissance man, left Dee open to challenge for many years as nothing more than a "conjuror."

At the point of leaving for an extended visit to Europe in 1583 at the invitation of Prince Albert Laski of Poland, Dee produced a catalog of his library. It is one of the first library catalogs known, and one which Yates claims to be an "absolutely basic document for the understanding, not only of Dee himself, but of the courtiers, noblemen, poets, scholars, scientists of the Elizabethan age for whom this was the best library in the country." It also gives us some notion of how the ordering of knowledge and its physical representation was taking form: "partially systematic though the system varies. Some . . . arranged according to size, others according to language . . . subject groupings, Paracelsist books (a large section), Lullist books, historical books, books of travel and discovery . . . . Nevertheless there is nothing haphazard about the catalogue; the entries are clearly written and usually include date and place of publication as well as author and title."[6]

Among the manuscript books in his library were five on the art of memory, and in his approach to books and knowledge Dee took what could now be perceived as a very modern stance. He was less concerned with how the books and manuscripts were physically arranged than with how their knowledge might be organized and retrieved in his mind. While obviously familiar with the various magical memory methods, Dee was not himself a memory system innovator. However, he helped set in place a role for libraries in preserving learning, enlarged the horizons for Elizabethan exploration by ship and mind, and promoted the new concepts of a Copernican universe—but one whose stars were very much numbered with ghosts and angels as well as the stones of the field.

Meanwhile, far to the south in Naples was Giordano Bruno, a young Dominican monk whose influence on European thought would far transcend even that of Dee's in England. Faced with charges of heresy, Bruno had broken from his monastic vocation and begun the travels that would carry his versions of Dominican memory systems, and his reframing of Copernican heliocentrism, to Geneva, Paris, London, and Prague.[7]

Copernicus had argued in his *De Revolutionibus Orbium Caelestium* (1543) that the Sun lay at the center of our universe, refuting the stubbornly maintained Ptolemaic concept of the Earth as the center of all things. But Copernicus believed the stars to be living, bright animals that prowled an outer circular sphere that sealed the universe within. Bruno was greatly affected by Copernicus's ideas, but went beyond them in his interpretations influenced by the writings ascribed to Hermes Trismegistus. These suggested the concept of an infinite universe to Bruno, an idea that was violently resisted by the church, but one that would fuel the new mathematics, the philosophies, and the sciences shortly to come.

Bruno's first two works, *De Umbris Idearum* and *Cantus Circaeus,* deal with his theories of magic memory but press far beyond mnemonics into solar magic and talismanic images, by which a thinker might bring those "shadows of ideas" in the archetypal heavens into his own consciousness: "If you embrace in your thought all things at once, times, places, substances, qualities, quantities, you may understand God."

The "ex-friar, infinitely wild, passionate, and unrestrained" (as Yates described him) published his ideas in Paris, solicited the favor of Henri III in the courts of France, then went to London in a rising tumult over his religion to seek the support of Elizabeth and address a challenge to "the most excellent Vice Chancellor of Oxford University and its celebrated doctors and teachers." Bruno argued for an animistic Copernican universe, but an infinite one. For two years he moved through the courtly and supper scenes of London, astounded audiences with memory feats, and published works sharply critical of the Oxford establishment. These writings were not intended to lead the unenlightened to a new age of science, but to redirect them to the elder magical religions. Bruno left his influence on the Sidney circles and returned to Paris, Prague, and other receptive cities on the Continent.

Eventually, Bruno and John Dee would both spend considerable time soliciting the patronage of Rudolf II of Poland, a supporter of studies of the occult. While they apparently never met—for Bruno was in England during two of the six years that Dee was in Europe—they would profoundly enlarge each other's influence, paving the way for a new science to spring from the magics they laid. While each solicited the support of the political rulers of the day, for no philosopher went far without political or theological blessings, each would suffer enormously from the reactions that came with every small intellectual advance.

Dee returned to England in 1589. His champion Philip Sidney was dead from a military foray to the Netherlands; Europe and England were stung by a series of hysterical witch-hunts; and Elizabeth's coming successor, James, the king of Scotland and author of *Daemonologie,* was violently damning anything ascribed to conjuration. Dee found his vast library and collection of scientific equipment vandalized, and lived his final years in the shadow of disfavor, reputedly selling his books off one by one for his dinners. Bruno foolishly returned to Italy, where he was secured by the Inquisition; spent eight years imprisoned under question; and on a cold February day in 1600 was ridden backwards on a mule, in a white robe, to Rome's Field of Flowers, where he was burned at the stake.

A Legacy of Memory Magic

Dee and Bruno each left behind in the works they composed, and in those persons within whom they inspired new dimensions of thought, a legacy of memory arts-based magic and knowledge systems no longer fettered by a finite, ecclesiastically defined universe. This influence clearly extended into the earliest years of the seventeenth-century advance when, as Yates has it, "the art of memory survive[d] as a factor in the growth of scientific method."[8]

Bacon, Descartes, and Leibniz (who respectively brought us the inductive method, analytical geometry, and a universal calculus) all spent their early days awash in the speculations of Dee and Bruno, considering the art of memory and how its reformation might influence the new methods from which modern science would so immediately blossom.

Francis Bacon (1561–1626), much in the tradition of the early memory arts, wrote of "prenotions" and "emblems" for place and image as a primitive form of classification in the investigation of natural science.

René Descartes (1596–1650) believed that the art of memory could provide "an easy way of making myself master of all I discovered through the imagination . . . that out of unconnected images should be composed new images common to them all, or that one image should be made which should have reference not only to the one nearest to it but to the all" (*Cogitationes Privatae*).

Gottfried Wilhelm Leibniz (1646–1716) introduced from the memory arts "characteristica," or significant signs or characters, as mathematical symbols; and he called images "notas" that could recall things or words to the calculating mind. The information system Leibniz envisioned was an encyclopedia that would bring together all the arts and sciences known to humankind, with "characters" assigned to all notions, and a universal calculus applied to retrieve this universe of knowledge and solve all problems.[9]

Leibniz even devised a calculating machine, but ultimately had to be satisfied with the library as the means for repositing knowledge. As Daniel Boorstin describes it, "Leibniz saw the library as a congregation of all knowledge with the librarian as minister keeping the congregation up-to-date and freely communicating. He pioneered in classification schemes, alphabetical finding aids, and abstracts to help the scholar. The library was his encyclopedia."[10]

So the magics were laid away, or became hidden in the rising arcana of Rosicrucianism. The new sciences and their methods flourished, and memory systems—finding no machine or the human mind capable alone of storing and retrieving knowledge as had been pursued by the magical memory brotherhood—surrendered the transmittal of knowledge to the formats and order that libraries grew to provide.

Frances Yates summarized the influence of the hermetic philosophers on the development of modern science and also moved towards prophecy when she observed in 1964 that "the Renaissance conception of an animistic universe, operated by magic, prepared the way for a mechanical universe, operated by mathematics . . . . Bruno's assumption that the astral forces which govern the outer world also operate within, and can be reproduced or captured there to operate a magical-mechanical memory seems to bring one curiously close to the mind machine which is able to do so much of the work of the human brain by mechanical means."[11]

Had Dame Frances been able to follow the development of the "mind machines" she found so curiously close to the memory systems of the Renaissance, and had she done so within the context of the information nova of the late twentieth century, she would have found other curious parallels between the knowledge systems and magics of two widely separated centuries.

Modern Magics/Scientific Complexity

As one construes things to be "supernatural" that lie outside the generally accepted definitions of present-day natural science, there is an increasing trend in the late twentieth century to achieve some supernatural handhold on current knowledge. One wants to employ fresh language and images as magical as any of the sixteenth century in the attempt to find new order in the structure and complexity of the natural world, to bring new dimensions to the sciences we know.

The information daemon, chaos, and new computational angels are evoked by today's most compelling thinkers to find fresh meaning and metaphors. The universe has become as clouded by doctrinal examination and representation as it was in the days before Renaissance philosophies broke heaven's spherical panes.

One does not ordinarily expect the word "chaos" to define an elegant order, but rather the random, the erratic, and the utter unpredictability of certain natural behaviors. Yet in the past decade a new science of chaos has offered a fresh approach, a new way of understanding the growth of complexity in nature. What several scientific disciplines could not discover from their traditional perspectives, new commonalities in the study of chaos are bringing thinkers together (as James Gleick describes) in rapidly "reshaping the fabric of the scientific society."[12]

Sir James Clerk Maxwell, the Scottish physicist who developed the equations governing electric and magnetic fields, posited a thermodynamic paradox in his book *Theory of Heat* (1870). Maxwell suggested a fantastical perpetual-motion device presided over by "a being whose faculties are so sharpened that he can follow every molecule in its course," an imp which was soon dubbed "Maxwell's demon." Maxwell's puzzle of energy creation took over half a century to resolve. Physicists still invoke the demon that early on had raised serious questions regarding the inviolability of the first and second laws of thermodynamics—that energy can neither be created nor destroyed, and that the entropy of any closed system can never decrease.

The science writer William Poundstone, in examining the state of information and structure in the universe, turned to Maxwell's "information demon" and a computer game, "Life," to help validate the overwhelming complexity and richness of a universe that defies any explanation of order within it.[13] Poundstone used the information demon to construct and review an imaginary Universal Video Library, defined to hold a copy of *every possible* videotape 100,000 frames long, with each pixel distinguished in all its individuality of color and degree of brightness. While there are no illogicalities in constructing such a library, the number of videotapes in such a collection can be calculated, and would far exceed the number of atoms in the observable universe, while any effort to locate recognizable objects in the tape library would yield nothing but video snow.

Chance is unable to explain the rich orderliness of the universe, Poundstone contends. He cites the work of the mathematician John von Neumann on computers and automata which supports the notion that machines can be self-creating and self-improving, that structures can grow richer under physical law.

Similarly, he observes that Claude Shannon, the founder of information theory, working from the similarities between thermodynamics and information, proved the growing entropy of information systems—an evolving information complexity derived from a simple, repeating transmittal code. To Poundstone, then, "Complexity is self-generating" and "Creation can be simple." A simple structure and basic physical laws established in a recursive (pattern-repeating) model would generate not only self-reproduction but also systems more complex than their parent. An information daemon and a computer game say it is so.

The whole field of physics is disquieted because the scientific method is no longer able to keep up with the conjurations of the day; observation can no longer confirm theory. Among some there is concern that the modern body of physics will crumble. Scientists contend in almost theological tones. Recently, in discussing this problem as it relates to "superstring theory" as a theoretical approach to understanding matter, the Nobel laureate Sheldon Glashow observed, "the historical connection between experimental physics and theory has been lost. Until the string people can interpret perceived properties of the real world, they simply are not doing physics. Should they be paid by universities and be permitted to pervert impressionable students? . . . . Are string thoughts more appropriate to departments of mathematics or even to schools of divinity than to physics departments? How many angels can dance on the head of a pin? How many dimensions are there in a compactified manifold thirty powers of ten smaller than a pinhead?"[14]

Until risk-takers make the effort to break the received tradition, there is never intellectual advance. The deeps of the universe, the boundaries of knowledge, the face of humankind have always been circumscribed by the conceptual limitations of the human mind. The thought model that opened the universe beyond the spheres of Copernicus paved the way for modern science. Dare anyone imagine that the shores on which contemporary science and philosophy have paused are the final beachheads of humankind's knowledge enterprise? Or, as Glashow says, "Can anyone really believe that nature's bag of tricks has run out?"

A New Orderliness in Libraries

A thought model that incorporates new electronic information formats, that employs new magics relating image and place to shape the new computations, and that defines a fresh vision of the universe, will open a way to the newer sciences undoubtedly to come. Again, as 400 years ago, the profound influences that are reshaping the contemporary knowledge world also have great potential for affecting the means by which libraries acquire, house, retrieve, relate, and display knowledge and information. Several library philosophers have begun a rethinking of traditional library programs and procedures in the light of new electronic information formats and the capabilities of the computer to refine the ordering of information, knowledge, and the contents of libraries. Libraries may, in fact, be more profoundly affected by new means of "relating" and "displaying" information than by any other changes occurring in the new knowledge world.

D. Kaye Gapen, in a talk to the American Library Association's Annual Conference in New Orleans on July 9, 1988, entitled "Impact of Technologies on Resource-Sharing, Linkages, Cooperation," described the changes in libraries "becoming information systems which address problems, which clarify problems, and which attack problems."[15] Gapen describes three ascending library paradigms in a conceptual model of change: the Library Warehouse Paradigm, an Electronic Information Paradigm, and a third paradigm which will exist, she asserts, by 1995, and that "will involve the creation of new Knowledge/Thought systems in which the human brain (which has been our primary information processing device) will be complemented by computer software which will allow not only the rapid storage and transfer of information, but also processing and representation of information in new and different ways."

"Hypertext is the first inkling . . . ," she says. "Having gained access to a point in the text you can use hypertext software to jump from point to point in the text, or between associated texts, through a web of associations." This will form the basis, Gapen asserts, for a synergistic networking of information sources, and a massive transformation of libraries and the information world.

Although the concept of hypermedia—the relating of words and sounds and images—has been with us for thirty years or so, computer software has only recently developed the hypertext capabilities that Gapen describes. The new capabilities are much like those systems the Renaissance memory artists believed would recollect and relate all things, because they will enable the accessing of all related information from any point of entry in a body of information associated by signs and locations. This leads, in turn, to new and striking possibilities.

First, I would suggest that we will move even more rapidly through hypertext concepts toward "hypersystems" in which knowledge and information systems themselves, not just information databases, will echo and reinforce one another toward more powerful accomplishments than any one system would allow alone. Traditional information systems—libraries, and their long-established programs and services—will be linked with any number of new "knowledge/thought" (information and computing) systems through open system interfaces. The result will be an enormous expansion of our capacities for storing, retrieving, representing, and manipulating information and, therefore, a new order of achievement in the age-old goal of generating new knowledge.

In the simplest of examples, the present scholarly information systems developing in research libraries represent "hyper" (or extended) relationships between the traditional library model (based on a book and journal collection, card catalogs, reference desk assistance, and interlibrary lending and other standard delivery services) and the heart of a rapidly permuting library system paradigm. Such a paradigm incorporates technologies and philosophies based on electronic information and computer assistance networked through campus computation centers and remote databases as well as the local library collection.

John Sculley of Apple Computer has described a future Information Navigator that will allow one to enter an information system at any point and travel throughout it on a hypertext basis, while Steve Jobs's NeXT Computer displays multitasking and multipath relationships that hint strongly at hypersystem concepts.

Hypersystems will magnify individual system capabilities in ways that will be technically reminiscent of the use of multiple parallel processors in computing, will promote the development of expert systems and artificial intelligence, and will allow for interactivity among knowledge and other systems in ways we cannot yet dream. Interestingly, the binary codes and icon-based commands of modern microcomputers are strikingly similar to the place and image concepts of sixteenth-century magical memory devices.

Second, and beyond the enormous potential of hypersystems to push us towards a new physics and theology of information, new prospects also appear promising for even the more mundane ordering and reordering of libraries themselves. These prospects are suggested in what appears to be a new approach to research librarianship.

The core of this approach lies in how the research library envisions its work, and especially in how it sees its relationship to research. Francis Miksa, a scholar of classification systems, has examined research patterns within the traditional universe of knowledge orientation of research libraries. He urges the adoption of a revised perspective on the research process that will more adequately provide for its support within the university. Technological innovation is not itself at the heart of the revised perspective, Miksa says, but rather an appreciation of several changes that have taken place in research itself: a shift toward more vigorous and sophisticated research methods, the professionalization of research, and "vastly different and more complex patterns of research information flow."[16]

These factors, and new patterns of research information flow, according to Miksa, not only make necessary a striking reordering of research libraries' collection development policies, but even more importantly the establishment of a demand-driven information acquisition and access process. The latter should be focused on "the point of need, rather than on the basis of long-range collecting plans that are themselves based on universe of knowledge parameters."

This rejection of the classic research library's worldview of collecting simply in order to represent a mythically stable universe of knowledge will also require the organization of collections on a highly distributed basis; the employment of highly specialized subject experts, themselves broadly distributed at the points where research is being done; and the retrieval of either *sign* or *text* as an option for the scholar.

In other words, the scholar might review either a subject listing (including a bibliographic citation with its attendant descriptive information regarding the text) or the text itself (in either an abstract or full-text version) before deciding to "acquire" the text through any of several types of delivery systems. Miksa suggests a "find out about" process and a "get" process—"bibliographic control at the source"—as a definition for this activity.

In a sense, the scholar makes a conscious choice of what is needed and what is not needed at both extremes of this search-and-retrieve process. Then a hypersystem process, it seems to me, would be applied to this model to help guide and move the user about in the knowledge system and to make selections throughout the information flow.

These points are all brought graphically into focus in a recent news story that describes a new class of microcomputer software that will dramatically extend the usefulness of personal computers, "programs known variously as daemons, sprites, phantoms, dragons or agents," which "computer scientists believe . . . will increasingly evolve into intelligent assistants for computer users." More specifically, with respect to libraries, the article describes a prospective national digital library that would use the concept of daemon programs and a "knowledge daemon" to provide access to a huge array of widely distributed databases, including technical information, card catalogs, and the text of research papers and periodicals, and enable a scholar "to find a document anywhere with a single command to a personal computer."[17]

A New Breed of Librarian

All of this calls for a new breed of scholar-librarians who will develop views of their world that are every bit as paradigm-shattering as those promoted by their Renaissance and seventeenth-century librarian colleagues, Dee and Leibniz. This is a new order of memory storage and retrieval systems within a knowledge/thought (hypersystem) paradigm. It will represent as significant an opportunity for a new orderliness in libraries as when knowledge was cast out of the monasteries to begin a journey toward different types of storage—toward magic memory retrieval. The result seeded the quickening of new sciences and human progress.

We have our own information daemon and memory magics to compare with the pseudosciences and mysteries of Shakespeare's time, in our quest to extend the capacity of the human mind, to relate knowledge, and to bring a new orderliness to libraries. Have we another Renaissance before us? I suspect we do, as new magics charm away traditional acceptations, as the universe rebuilds its recursive richness of human ingenuity, as libraries gather and order human knowledge in new electronic book chests, when the hurly-burly's done.

NOTES

1. Frances A. Yates, *The Art of Memory* (Chicago: University of Chicago Press, 1966). Virtually no research had been done in English on the history of the memory arts and their role in the development of

modern thought and science until Frances Amelia Yates began serious historical study in the field about 1940. For her extensive body of work on the Renaissance, she was made a member of the Order of the British Empire in 1972 and was awarded the Wolfson Prize for historical writing in 1973.

2. Yates, *Art of Memory,* 127–28.

3. John Crowley, "Shakespeare's Ghosts," in *The Penguin Encyclopedia of Horror and the Supernatural,* ed. Jack Sullivan (New York: Viking, 1986), 377–79. Crowley, a superb American fabulist, has begun a series of novels based on the mystical lives of Dee and Bruno, the first of which is *Aegypt* (Toronto, New York: Bantam, 1987).

4. Elmer D. Johnson, *History of Libraries in the Western World,* 2nd ed. (Metuchen, N.J.: Scarecrow, 1970).

5. Frances A. Yates, *Theatre of the World* (Chicago: University of Chicago Press, 1969), 5.

6. Yates, *Theatre,* 10.

7. Frances A. Yates, *Giordano Bruno and the Hermetic Tradition* (Chicago: University of Chicago Press, 1964).

8. Yates, *Art of Memory,* 369.

9. Ibid., 368–69.

10. Daniel Boorstin, *The Discoverers* (New York: Random House, 1983), 535.

11. Yates, *Art of Memory,* 225.

12. James Gleick, *Chaos: Making a New Science* (New York: Viking, 1987).

13. William Poundstone, *The Recursive Universe: Cosmic Complexity and the Limits of Scientific Knowledge* (New York: Morrow, 1985), 52–77, 90–102.

14. Sheldon Glashow, "Tangled in Superstring: Some Thoughts on the Predicament Physics Is In," *The Sciences* 28 (May–June 1988): 25.

15. D. Kaye Gapen, "Impact of Technologies on Resource-Sharing, Linkages, Cooperation," unpublished paper read at the American Library Association's Annual Conference, New Orleans, July 9, 1988.

16. Francis Miksa, *Research Patterns and Research Libraries* (Dublin, Ohio: OCLC, 1987).

17. John Markoff, "For PC's, a New Class of Software," *New York Times,* March 8, 1989, sec. Y, p. 34.

3

~~~

Governing Library Networks
The Quick and the Dead for the 1990s

Networking is one of the most pervasive terms and themes to enter the library field—and beyond—during the past twenty years. There are radio program "Talknets," the daily paper describes the week's astronomical events in "SkyNet," and social needs are addressed through a Staff Parents Network. We now "network" libraries, computers, databases, terminals, and friends from management summer camp. Where libraries once joined with one another in cooperative organizations or consortia, they now connect through networks.

The distinction, of course, is that members of contemporary organizations are more generally linked through common telecommunications and computing facilities that facilitate resource sharing and the pursuit of common programmatic and service objectives. New patterns of relationships and governance in research library networking must evolve if the successes of recent years are to carry into the next decade.

An Explosion of Networks

Cooperative organizations have existed for many years in the research library community. For example, the North Carolina Union Catalog was established in the early 1930s, the Association of Research Libraries in 1932, and the Center for Research Libraries in 1945. The

---

This article was originally published in *Library Journal* 114 (November 1, 1989).

past twenty years, however, have seen a virtual explosion of library cooperative networks as computers and telecommunications entered the library scene. Of special significance among these was the formation of the Ohio College Library Center (OCLC) in 1967 and the Research Libraries Group (RLG) in 1974. (The OCLC's name was changed to Online Computer Library Center in 1981.)

The establishment of the OCLC also provided a significant base from which ancillary library networks have sprung since 1973, initially with the thought that such regional or state organizations would replicate the OCLC's systems. That anticipated role changed to one of serving primarily as brokers for the provision of OCLC services when it became clear that fiscal and technical constraints made replication a virtual impossibility.

In 1989 there were nineteen state and regional networks in the United States, as well as several new agencies abroad that contracted to provide OCLC services and support to some 9,000 participating libraries in this and twenty-six other countries. This plethora of network development was enormously important to libraries in earlier years in constructing a means for cooperative computerized library services. Recently it may have turned into so many albatrosses hung about the necks of individual libraries and the "national" library network.

Competing to Replicate the OCLC

Since no individual library in the early 1970s could easily finance or develop systems comparable to those of the OCLC, libraries turned to community efforts to attempt replication of the OCLC's systems or to access its services. Cooperative organizations were able to leverage relatively small fiscal commitments from many libraries to accomplish what none could afford alone. Large groups of multitype libraries banded together on state or regional bases to organize and incorporate library network organizations with central offices and staffs to provide computerized programs and services.

It was not surprising that not only did the RLG and OCLC develop competitive positions, but that most of the network hatchlings of the OCLC developed strongly competitive and, at times, hostile relations with the mother agency. After all, the marketplace was the same, the basic bibliographic services provided were the same, and each organization needed a secure financial base for its operations.

The initial efforts of libraries and librarians in network development were very much ones of organization building. Large amounts of individual effort, institutional resources, and personal pride and commitment went into the work of getting library networks created. Little attention, however, was given to providing for the inevitable changing of organizations, or, indeed, for their eventual dissolution.

It is not surprising to find that as events have led to the need to review the mission, the governance structure, and even the raison d'être of organizations, there has been a great reluctance among libraries to do what clearly needs to be done—change organizations, or even dissolve them.

Built-In Resistance to Change

Not only is there a natural emotional resistance to such change in organizations we have worked so hard to build, but the very structure and corporate charters of networks were formalized in a manner that makes it difficult to change them. Take the OCLC and the regional networks that provide its services. Conceived, for the most part, as multitype library membership organizations, most regional networks consist of every conceivable type and size of library. There are small public or special libraries. There are medium-sized academic libraries and very large research libraries. There are private and public-supported institutions.

No formal power structures, either in the parent organization itself or in the regional networks that provide its services, represent the special interests of members—although a few networks, and some nomination committees, try to make the organization's governing body more representative through election processes. Generally, however, if a small public library is represented in the formal process, it is by accident. If a major research library is represented, it is by accident. If a medical library is represented, it is by accident.

Since each library represents one vote in the determination of organizational decisions, the heaviest contributor to the fiscal well-being of the organization has no more formal influence than the most infrequent of users. In formal membership actions there is the likelihood that smaller institutions, which constitute the large majority of the membership, can easily carry the vote on issues that may or may not be of equal relevance to other institutions of differing size, type, or interest.

The power of individual persuasion, or the combined accidents of election processes—both driven by the philosophy and strength of network directors and staff—provide the network decision-making processes.

As technological and fiscal forces have affected the network scene over the past fifteen years, it has been increasingly difficult to maintain a congruence of agreement among the highly varied institutional membership of regional networks. The perception among many research library directors is that regional networks no longer speak as directly to contemporary research library needs as they once did.

Susan K. Martin, who has contributed several helpful works on networks, has commented on this issue:

> The role and impact of the governance structure cannot be under-estimated . . . the boards of directors, representing and elected by the membership, create the direction of the network, formulate policy, determine the posture of the network toward the outside world and decide what financial investment the members should make in the network . . . the early active participants were the large libraries . . . and the directors of major libraries were often the founders and the original guides of the networks . . . [while] current boards . . . tend to be a mixture of directors of medium-sized and smaller libraries and lower level administrative staff from the larger libraries. By defi-nition, the perspective of the boards differs from that of the early pio-neering years.[1]

Martin goes on to say, "Strangely, the library profession appears to be-lieve that while governance was an issue at one time, the concerns of the late 1970s have been resolved. Nothing could be further from the truth."

When the heavy demand for OCLC services drew that organiza-tion beyond the Ohio borders in the mid-1970s, the consulting firm of Arthur D. Little was commissioned to develop recommendations for a new OCLC governance structure more appropriate to that organiza-tion's evolving national role. This led to a reorganization of the cor-poration in 1977. The governance structure chosen reflected a tightly held corporation with a small governing board (of whom a significant number of members had to be drawn from outside the library field) and a large elected Users Council intended to reflect the larger membership as it was constituted within the numerous regional networks brokering OCLC services.

Out-of-Date Governance

In effect, there was no model for the governance of an organization such as the OCLC in 1977. Arthur D. Little invented the structure. At the time, none of the broader changes that might require changes in the organizational structure were foreseen. Some of these changes include the subsequent technological revolution, the OCLC's move "beyond bibliography" to provide broader information-based services, and the competition in the information industry in which the OCLC finds itself. In addition, the OCLC embarked upon the international initiatives that made it operative in twenty-seven countries. Service began to new user groups including individual scholars and researchers, and the globalization of information and other changes in modern society occurred at a very rapid pace. None of these things was foreseen in 1977 when the Arthur D. Little recommendations were accepted and implemented.

The governance nexus in which the Board of Trustees, the Users Council, the OCLC management, the networks, the libraries themselves both singly and in their special interest groups, and other interested parties find themselves does not reflect today's realities nor those projected for the future. How can a "membership" organization of 9,000 libraries in several dozen countries best represent the OCLC's constituency and work collaboratively toward common goals?

The strategic forces at work on the OCLC during the past ten years have also had their effect on the state and regional networks providing OCLC services, as well as on the Research Libraries Group and its supporting technical system, the Research Libraries Information Network (RLIN). Among these forces have been the increasing installation of local systems and the establishment of numerous local and several new statewide networks.

There is also the growing distribution of library computing and processing functions, the burgeoning availability of information in new electronic formats, and the general internationalization of libraries. The rapid move of libraries outside their previous physical confines and into the broader fields of scholarly communication and research is another such force, along with the considerably reduced fiscal ability of libraries to deal with these changes.

The Return to Local Systems

Richard De Gennaro has written perceptively on the factors driving libraries toward decentralization. "The interest, energy, and resources that went into network building in the 1970s," De Gennaro says, "are now going into buying and installing mini- and microcomputer-based local systems with particular emphasis on the local online public access catalog and retrospective conversion."[2]

"The 1980s will be dominated by a return to local systems," he wrote in 1983. Since virtually any library now has the capability to acquire a microcomputer and bibliographic records on compact disk, along with software that will provide for a local online catalog as well as support automated acquisitions and serials control systems, the national utilities that libraries once had to rely on are at great risk.

As De Gennaro correctly predicted, "The general euphoria in favor of cooperation and networking that characterized the 1970s is over . . . . The networks are going to have to compete with local systems and commercial vendors in the 1980s or they will lose their members and their financial base."

Also at risk in this developing scenario of distributed systems, numerous local networks, and potentially crumbling regional network services is the virtual national library network. The national library network is the electronic linkage of bibliographic records and library holdings that has provided for the sharing of library cataloging and of library materials through automated interlibrary lending systems.

The fact is, of course, that the OCLC Online Union Catalog has been the de facto national network. The sheer size and diversity of its database, membership, holdings locations, and transactional activity make it so.

By contrast, the RLIN, the computer network that supports the various cooperative programs of the RLG—while national in geographical scope—is purposefully aimed at a selective, smaller group with a different design and different functions at its heart. Unlike the OCLC, for instance, the RLIN system has more locally supported the technical processing of member libraries and provides direct access to each library's own bibliographic records, as well as serving as the technical vehicle for the RLG's programs.

It might be anticipated that the RLG would be the initial network to suffer the serious effects of distributed processing, since its community of users is so much smaller than the OCLC's, and a move by members from the RLIN to local systems would be more quickly and heavily felt. The OCLC would be buffered to some extent by the sheer size of its membership and transactional activities. But if its chief contributors, the major research libraries, moved too quickly to local systems, it too could be hurt by a loss of revenue and bibliographic records.

Strongly Separated Camps

Neither network can long withstand the retreat of its supporting institutions to local systems unless those institutions make special commitments to the ongoing health and stability of the utilities and the virtual national network. The two networks continue to exist in strongly separated camps at the very time when they stand in most need of fresh cooperative ventures to seize the opportunities presented by the new technologies, as well as protection against the inroads of the erosive forces already mentioned.

The Research Libraries Group was established in 1974 as a partnership of libraries and parent universities—not just the libraries. Originally consisting of the New York Public Library and the libraries of Columbia, Harvard, and Yale universities, the consortium was formed to solve collaboratively the special problems of large research libraries. Recognizing the need for a single integrated technical system to support the programs of the consortium, the group moved in 1978 to adapt the BALLOTS system of Stanford (in preference to the OCLC or other systems) and renamed it RLIN.

Harvard chose to leave the membership, the RLG was reorganized to include Stanford, and other research libraries soon joined. From its original membership of four institutions in 1974, the membership of the RLG had grown to thirty-six by 1988, with a number of additional associate or special members utilizing special RLG programs or services.[3]

It seems apparent that if the Association of Research Libraries (ARL) had not grown so large and disparate in 1974, and if it had had a more solid programmatic base and the capability of adopting a common technical-support system, there might well have been no perceived need for an RLG. The technical and programmatic separation of the ARL's member libraries into OCLC and RLIN user groups over the past ten years has clearly worked against a more orderly and unified frame of research library activities within the ARL.

As "owner/members" of the single-type library organization, the Board of Trustees of the RLG functions as a committee of the whole, one library–one vote, but distributes its governance somewhat, and makes it more effective, through the establishment of a function-oriented committee structure. This stands in sharp contrast to the large multitype library membership and governance structures of the OCLC and the various state and regional networks where, as has already been pointed out, the type of library or other criteria plays no part in formal decision-making processes. Both Martin and De Gennaro have commented that the large size of the utilities poses a threat to their effective governance.

Stay with the OCLC or Migrate to the RLIN?

Interestingly, soon after the reorganization of the OCLC in 1977, there was a move towards special-interest representation within the OCLC despite the lack of a formal means to accomplish this in its corporate structure. The RLG helped bring this about through its own membership-building initiatives. A number of research libraries migrated from the OCLC to the RLG after the latter's reorganization in 1978. Other OCLC members resisted what was perceived to be overly strong pressure to join the RLG consortium.

In early 1980 a group of these OCLC members formed the Research Libraries Advisory Committee to OCLC (RLAC) "to articulate the particular needs and concerns of research libraries in OCLC and communicate these needs and concerns to the managing and governing bodies of OCLC." Other special-interest groups were soon formed within the OCLC but lying outside its formal governance structure.

In the end, many research libraries simply chose not to migrate from the OCLC system to the RLIN. They felt that their investment in the OCLC was too deep, that too many questions surrounded the fiscal or technical stability of the RLG, or that the programmatic opportunities lying within the ARL provided means enough for libraries to work collaboratively towards solving common problems.

Another important issue was the perceived worldview of the RLG- or OCLC-based networks. These differences may be traced to the contrasting genesis of the two groups. The RLG was born out of the common interests of a very small, deliberately limited group of private eastern institutions. Its economic implications were initially seen as negligible. As a group the RLG later sought a connecting technology. The OCLC, on the other hand, was born from populist roots in the state of Ohio, and soon became a technology looking for a wider group. The economic implications of system maintenance were obvious, and building a broad membership and financial base was mandated.

The RLG was seen in a particularly critical light by many institutions, especially in the initial construction. It was characterized as an overly insular approach to the problems of research libraries: the joining of a group of "elite" institutions into an inward-looking, last redoubt against the problems of the library world. The efforts of this organization to secure operating capital and pursue a common mission—its members working together regularly and closely within particular programmatic boundaries in highly structured committees—led to a strong bonding process, especially among its earlier members.

The building of the OCLC and the regional networks, by contrast, could be seen as a very populist effort, within the frame of state-supported institutions and multitype library bonding. It was seen as an extraordinarily (and perhaps extravagantly) democratic and outward-looking network-building effort that reached for as many institutional members as possible, never mind their diversities or the inherent governance problems described earlier.

To some RLG members, the reluctance of major OCLC institutions to join their RLG colleagues in common programmatic pursuits within the RLIN system was seen as frustrating and as emotionally charged with the attitude of those institutions that characterized the RLG as "elite." Nevertheless, the idea of abandoning their commitment to fellow state institutions and network members by migrating from the OCLC to the RLG seemed particularly troublesome to large public research libraries.

This basic philosophic difference in how the RLG and OCLC communities were formed, and in their worldview, has probably continued to separate the groups more than any other single issue. As will be seen, the orientation of these organizations has undergone significant changes in recent years and accounts for much of the current fraternal tension that urges a closer association of the two while also fostering their continuing separation and competitive posture.

The Drive to Restructure

Given a perceived diminution of research library influence in the OCLC's governance; a number of continuing threats to the OCLC and its research constituency (the proliferation of local systems, for example); and what appears to be a fresh opportunity to bring the larger community of research libraries into closer harmony, the Research Libraries Advisory Committee to OCLC recently petitioned the OCLC's Board of Trustees to review its organizational structure.

While recognizing that there are a number of other stakeholders in the OCLC, its research library members have noted that the level of their contributions to the OCLC, the level of products and services they use, and their stake in the future of the OCLC mandate that their institutions, their faculty, and their libraries play a major role in the OCLC and have a powerful voice in its management and governance. It has been suggested that a new Arthur D. Little–type study might help define the most effective governance structure for the OCLC in new and volatile circumstances.

The seeds for change in the worldview of the RLG were planted when it was reorganized in 1978. More recent additions to its membership have tended to come from libraries that had been members of the regional networks and had gone through the more populist network-building and bonding experience. These libraries carried a more outward-looking view than that of the RLG's original members, which had a completely different focus in mind when they set out to establish a small community of like institutions to join in mutual problem solving and resource sharing.

In fact, a number of new RLG member institutions maintained their memberships in both organizations on joining the RLG and carry less historical investment in the RLG's founding standpoint. In recent months several RLG members have relinquished their full partnership status in that organization.

Another key to changing positions can be related to Richard De Gennaro's observations on the influence of present trends towards distributed processing and the force of "economic stresses to face reality." The long history of the RLG's reliance on grants and gifts suggests that its organizational ambition has exceeded its fiscal reach. An organization whose programs are so interwoven with its technical system simply must have the capital to renew its technological base.

Martin, too, has recently observed that a lack of sufficient resources is constraining the support of full central systems while libraries also implement their own local systems: "Librarians are in the process of attempting to identify how to strip down the huge networks they have built to a size that appears to be affordable in the context of local systems."[4]

Given the severe economic strain of recent years on their home institutions and a comparative thinning of federal and other support, there is simply no longer any financial margin in the nation's research libraries to duplicate programs or systems.

Thus, virtually every tide, from economics to ideological orientation, is turning research libraries toward more common ground and a fresh look at network relations. Unfortunately, the existing governance structures are not helping this process.

No Governance Models

Just as there was no model for the governance of an organization such as the Online Computer Library Center in 1977, there is now no governance model for such an organization as the OCLC has become. Just as the OCLC's first twenty years cannot determine the next twenty, neither should the governance structure of the past decade dictate that for the next. What is needed is an effective governance structure for the future. Clearly, any technologically driven network should have the flexibility to act entrepreneurially and promptly in times of rapid change and perishable opportunities.

The committee-as-a-whole board of the RLG allows for more flexible and responsive action than the OCLC, although the size of that board and the constitution of its membership are not what were originally intended. Any consideration of proposals for blending the research library interests, programs, services, and technical support of these organizations raises major questions of relational models and governance. Regardless of what type of network might arise from the present circumstances, it must have an effective governance structure for the future.

The imposition of a national information policy or schema to bring order to our networks, to the national flow of information, and to the growth of knowledge was a consideration early in the decade, but that concept seems fortunately to have been cast aside. Don R. Swanson has argued persuasively against a monolithic structure, and has suggested instead a philosophy of progress based on the encouragement of innovation and entrepreneurial evolution.[5] It could then be argued that within a pluralistic, national "network of networks," progress would proceed through a mechanism of variation and selection in the information marketplace. Some "units" might die whenever a failure occurred, but not the whole system. The marketplace, as it were, would provide librarians with "a better method for knowing whether a service is dead or alive."

The concept of a national OCLC research libraries network has been discussed for a number of years, but OCLC research libraries (at least as represented by RLAC statements) have shied away from the concept, perhaps afraid that the establishment of such an organization would have detrimental effects on the regional networks in which they figure large. RLG interests have similarly focused on habitual relationships: the building and strengthening of a tightly knit network of libraries and universities. The technical and economic issues touched upon earlier may now well force a change in these attitudes.

It is conceivable that a new organizational bridge would allow research libraries to share a single technical system and participate in common-interest programmatic areas. If individual institutions found this desirable, it would move these long-separated camps into a new and badly needed era of cooperation. The national network would be preserved and new horizons of collaborative opportunity could be facilitated within the ARL.

Cooperation through Preservation

Preservation is an especially attractive area to serve as a common program-base for members of both organizations, with the RLG prospectively responsible for program management and the OCLC providing the technical-support system. From such a proto-effort a single national research library network might well arise.

What would be the effects of such change on regional networks? They are already under the gun from the establishment of many new local networks, as well as from the development of new statewide programs encouraged by funds made available by state agencies holding the overly optimistic view that library fiscal problems can be solved through extended resource-sharing programs.

In a reorganization of networked large research libraries, revenue would certainly be redistributed, although major libraries might well choose to continue their participation in regional or state networks for good benefit. A clear area of necessary, ongoing responsibility for these groups lies in a solid, generic brokering and training role for the provision of automated services to medium and small libraries. Many research libraries can also benefit from broader resource-sharing programs among their colleagues of all types and sizes.

Hugh Atkinson, in his typically pragmatic and populist way, said, "It is not necessary for outcomes, products, and uses of networks to be the results of an equal system, but rather that the network be valuable to each of the participants."[6] This presumes, of course, that a network is fiscally viable and that each participant can indeed afford the cost of a particular need that the network satisfies.

Strategic forces have probably pressed regional networks past the point of choosing whether to change or not. Some organizations may well be lost in the shakedown that is clearly under way, some have already made major accommodations to be more effective in the new information environment, and others must change if they are to remain viable. All must alter their governance structures if they hope to continue as effective, responsive organizations.

Toward an Effective Structure

What is needed in an effective network governance structure? Any organization should reflect in its structure the mission for which it was established. It must contain or represent

the special interests of its membership;

the flexibility to deal with technological, computing, and other change; and

the continuing capacity to renew itself in a new image most consonant with the future.

If network governance mechanisms do not allow for change and evolution within the corporate structure, I have no doubt that such organizations will die. Of course, it may be years before libraries that support them realize that they are paying for principles and dreams that were once vital but are now moribund in a dramatically changed world.

Where are the quick and the dead in the present national scene?

I have tried to point out some of the forces that are affecting the futures of the OCLC, the RLG, and the regional networks, and where those winds are driving these organizations. After a few relatively quiet years following the OCLC-Network Copyright Wars, the national scene has entered a new period of turmoil. Our fragile house of electronic cards is increasingly vulnerable. The ARL, OCLC, and RLG have all recently appointed new executive directors, all of whom are rethinking their organizations' responsibilities in the research library resource-sharing infrastructure that has been constructed in such delicate cooperative balance over the past twenty years.

The Library of Congress (whose supportive role in national resource-sharing efforts is so critically important) has a new Librarian who holds significant concerns about the LC's fiscal position in this balance, including questions about the desirability of an open door to the LC's Machine-Readable Cataloging (MARC) records. The implementation of recommendations from the LC's recently completed Management and Planning Study could have significant impact on research libraries—and on most other libraries as well, through our trickle-down national bibliographic economy.

A half dozen major research library directors' appointments have recently been made, and many other recruiting efforts are now in progress. Several leadership changes have also been made in the regional networks. Fresh councils, caucuses, and formal meetings are being heard of regularly—and research libraries seem intent on seeking a new mechanism to reunite them. There will be no quick but only the dead in the national resource-sharing superstructure if these stresses are not relieved and the uneasy balance fails.

Despite the overwhelming strategic effects on libraries that one would have expected from rapidly mutating technologies, constrained resources, and changing higher educational themes in recent times, it should be recalled that three or four strong and visionary individuals pretty well set research library directions for the past twenty years—and a handful of common networking efforts have sustained the drive. Leadership is highly important in establishing a course and directing strategic forces to desired ends. Governance is paramount to successful organizational networking. The tools to forge an exciting new library future are at hand if research libraries can find the leadership and a governance model to move them.

NOTES

1. Susan K. Martin, *Library Networks, 1986–87: Libraries in Partnership* (White Plains, N.Y.: Knowledge Industry Publications, 1986).
2. Richard De Gennaro, "Library Automation and Networking Perspectives on Three Decades," *Library Journal* 108 (April 1, 1983): 629–35.
3. By 2002 the RLG had become an international organization, with a membership of over 160 universities, national libraries, archives, historical societies, and other institutions with specialized holdings for research and learning. The organization had moved from its early focus on programmatic support for research libraries into an important niche as a developer and provider of specialized information resources with a market beyond its member group.
4. Susan K. Martin, "Technology and Cooperation: The Behaviors of Networking," *Library Journal* 112 (October 1, 1987): 42–44.
5. Donald R. Swanson, "Evolution, Libraries, and National Information Policy," *Library Quarterly* 50 (January 1980): 76–93.
6. Hugh C. Atkinson, "Atkinson on Networks," *American Libraries* 18 (June 1987): 432.

4

~~~~~

The Bionic Library

News of the revolution has finally arrived. After several cycles of reduced acquisitions by academic libraries, much of it in response to rapidly rising prices of journals, scholars nationwide are finally realizing that a national information crisis is at hand.

The journal problem is, of course, simply a part of the total information system concern. It reflects an increase in scholars and scholarship, the continually growing rush of information and knowledge, the devastation wrought by inflation, dollar devaluation, and at least a few greedy publishers, and the insidious diminishment of financial support for higher education.[1]

The growing distance between the quantity of literature produced and the capability of academic libraries to acquire it affirms that the battle for collection comprehensiveness has already been lost. The academic research library model has been changed forever.

There is reason for hope, however. Electronic information is a garden ready to flower, particularly if it will move towards a new distribution, use, and payment paradigm. To some scholars, the concept of an electronic library is paradise at hand; to others it is absolutely terrifying. I suggest that libraries are evolving as bionic libraries: organic, evolutionary, and electronically enhanced.

This article was originally published in *Library Journal* 116 (October 15, 1991).

Library collections will continue, perdurable with books and journals, but for some information sources available via remote workstations, the library will soon never sleep and electronic information will always be, so to speak, "on the shelf." The old and the new library systems will, in time, become assimilated and intertwined.

The Access Tantalus

If these are the worst of times for our collections, they are the best of times for access. Scholars have greater access to more information than ever before. Bibliographers were once fishers casting for information at night on an unlit sea. The printed *National Union Catalog* and *Union List of Serials*—glorious aids in their day—were woefully slow and inadequate tools compared to those now available.

During the past fifteen years, information resources have been illuminated by our networked utilities so that access to millions of titles is rapidly available to our information nets. But this access is chiefly bibliographic, not textual. Clearly, the major issue before us in this area of information gathering rests in the matter of delivery.

Technology offers not only improved access but also new means of delivery and representation. In a few minutes at a workstation, using the simple commands of a HyperFTP (file transfer protocol) system, one can bring image and full-text files over the Internet to one's desktop, comprehending with as much astonishment as Cortez viewing the Pacific that a new, virtual information universe is at hand. Whether the information received is the image of a Walt Disney character or a NASA space photo, text from a Yeats poem or the Bible, the practicality and the promise of electronic information delivery from remote information servers are clear.

Thus far, however, more attention has been paid to the highways for carrying information than has been addressed to the road signs that should tell us which highway will carry us to our information destination, to the packaging of information to be carried along those networked roads, or to the equipment to get us there and back again. But this is changing.

Too much importance has been attached to the ability to keyword search the entire text of articles. Such capability currently requires, for documents not already available on tape, time-consuming manual rekeying of text. A simple method of conversion is to scan the text and store it as optical images. Contents—if not already indexed—can be identified through files of tables of contents and index terms. For most articles, indexing of every word is not necessary, or even desirable. Nonetheless, either method offers hope for resolving the journal problem.

Electronic journals will never completely replace printed journals, any more than television replaced motion pictures. Relatively few of the 10,000–30,000 journal subscriptions currently received by each of the nation's academic research libraries exist in both print and digitized versions. Virtually no journal titles are now being converted from print to an all-electronic format, although the recent contents of about 2,000 journal titles have been converted into ASCII character format for computerized availability through commercial sources. While a few dozen new all-electronic journals have appeared, they are being created at the very margins of scholarship, generally as labors of love by their editors.

Information firms are just beginning to make more of the basic body of journal literature available in electronic format. A new service allows the user to retrieve the full texts of journal articles via an index to a networked "jukebox" of hundreds of compact disks containing optical images of the actual articles. While this system represents a significant advance, it still incorporates the limitations of CD-ROM technology—one access per disk at a time.

Subscribers to other electronic content services will receive information on a hard disk. Updates are then provided on CD-ROMs for downloading onto the computer file. A telecommunications link will allow searchers to request a copy of a document that could be supplied via interlibrary loan or a document delivery service. The intent is to move from a stopgap paper document system to electronic delivery.

The most exciting efforts in the area of electronic text generation and distribution are being carried out in places that are mom-and-pop operations in comparison to these large information technology companies. In several academic computing centers, computing staff and scholars have joined hands to produce and make accessible over the Internet a wide variety of electronic files. These include such well-known efforts as Project Gutenberg at the University of Illinois (with a goal of converting 10,000 of the most-used books to electronic text by the year 2000) and Dartmouth's Dante Project (a searchable database of six centuries of commentary on Dante's *Divine Comedy*), as well as hundreds of similar efforts around the globe.[2] A survey of the electronic text enterprise, a description of the technological changes associated with it, and a vision of an electronic library future have been brilliantly presented in an article by Reva Basch.[3]

The Information Flow

The information flow is becoming increasingly complex. Its forms, the windows to it, the resources that pay for it, the means to find it, evaluate it, and eventually retrieve, display, and process it will become increasingly multifarious and variegated for the users who require it.

The information flow process consists of the creation of information by authors, editors, translators, publishers, sponsors, composers, artists, directors, producers, and a host of others. It includes the consignment of information to different media (physical or digital) and a variety of formats (printed books, electronic journals, microforms, audio, video, graphics, and so on); access, which can be bibliographic or textual, and includes the act of "finding out about," of evaluating and identifying; and transfer, the process of display or "getting" for eventual processing.

Information does not become important until a user needs it. Its location prior to the user's need is of little consequence. What is important is convenient access to appropriate information when it is needed, the ability of the user to discriminate among a variety of sources in order to decide what is most pertinent, and the capability to transfer that information to the scholar for display and processing when it is needed, where it is needed, in whatever format is most useful.

It is important that librarians understand the whole of this process and help shape the flow of information. Librarians should be able to take the hand of the information seeker and step into the knowledge stream to help find, evaluate, and get whatever is needed. Just as two sets of steering wheels are used by airplane copilots or driving instructors so that one user may assist the other, librarians are beginning to consider remote reference assistance whereby the librarian can join a user on request in the midstream of a computerized information search or processing routine, assisting the user electronically hand in hand. Computer professionals are already accustomed to sharing a workstation-processing environment.

The library and information professional must be a fundamental and vital participant in this new information environment or abdicate that leadership to others. The library user who ignores the changes in the knowledge environment does so at great scholarly risk.

Understanding the Economics

The dynamics of information flow and its technology may be of less significance to us in solving the information crisis than its economics. As Nancy Eaton, while director of the Iowa State University Library, correctly observed, "Economic forces will shape the future library more than either user needs or evolving information technology."[4]

In romancing the flow—reviewing with exaggerated attention and careful detail—it is important to remember that we are playing by constantly changing rules; the old rules will not help. We need to identify the agencies involved, identify the currency (resources) of exchange, and, most importantly, identify the exchange points where resource transactions are made to propel information through the flow.

Agencies include authors, publishers, libraries, computing centers, research groups, scholarly and professional associations, bookstores, jobbers, subscription agents, bookbinders, and other individuals and organizations distributed throughout the information flow. The currency of exchange includes the costs and rewards to each agency. These can include economic considerations for the author. British and European models (wherein authors are paid for library circulation of their works) might be examined in regard to making possible changes in American reimbursement of authors. Appropriate consideration must be given to intellectual property rights, not only to compensate the rights holder and protect the integrity of the work, but also to promote scholarship and knowledge. The foundations of copyright and the publishing process are at issue here.

Costs and compensation to other agencies must be considered, among them publishers or other information distributors, the library or other information provider (subscription costs, costs of the acquisition process, record keeping, claiming, binding, preservation, security-stripping, housing, circulation, and so on; capital costs, operational costs, computing and telecommunication costs, collection costs versus transactional costs, site licenses), and costs to the user.

In the tradition of open and "free" access for the user to library resources, shall libraries increasingly absorb transaction costs and in the process forego capital collections, or shall such costs be transferred to the user? If libraries begin charging the user, what can we do to avoid creating an information lower class?

New Ways to Pay

Exchange points are found throughout the information flow wherever resources are exchanged. Every possible exchange point must be identified where resource bridges can be rebuilt for a more effective system.

Consider a few questions relating to possible changes at exchange points. What will happen to the campus bookstore if textbooks become available through the campus information system? CD-ROM services represent major cost centers along the interchange with rather limited access: must they soon be reengineered to enlarge their networking availability so that more users can use the same disk at the same time, or should their contents be shifted into local online information systems or remotely available computer-based service centers? The redeployment of advertising revenue from a traditional exchange point to another is an interesting consideration; advertising is vital to many commercial publishers as well as to the whole marketing structure. What happens if journals lose their advertising through conversion to an electronic format? What might happen if electronic publications from university or other nonprofit "publishers" received corporate sponsorship or advertising support—like public broadcasting?

The means of redistributing resources throughout the flow probably requires more dependence on a payment-for-use paradigm. Information access by transaction is a market virtually waiting to explode—a consumer-driven market that can better feed authors and publishers, as well as allow libraries to reduce some of the present huge costs of journal subscriptions and monographic acquisitions and the unseen overheads that support paper-based library collections.

Moving to transaction-based charges will enable libraries to begin chipping away at the present journals' thrall, redistributing some of the massive sums that are consumed by serial costs, to help leverage alternative means of information access.

One must look at the human and organizational requirements for change if a solution to the information crisis is to be wrenched from the current system. Bold librarians, scholarly publishers, and other information and computing specialists must look for new models of common effort that break old patterns and habits.

Mechanisms for Change

Libraries must do more to force these initiatives. If a collegium of libraries and scholarly publishers would join in the replacement of paper subscriptions with the storage of bit-mapped page images to be accessed and paid for on a site license or per transaction fee, much of the scenario envisioned above would take shape: libraries could begin redistributing the basic costs and operational overheads associated with some journal subscriptions throughout the information infrastructure. They could gain flexibility to acquire additional publications, to access other information, and perhaps to direct more revenue towards both publishers and authors and subsidize the information-deprived. Publishers must also join in this process. Where are the information giants who can smell the profits from investing in this change?

Some brave libraries have begun the transformation. Cornell University is involved with the Xerox Corporation, with support from the Commission on Preservation and Access (CPA), to develop a scanning, image-storage, and print-based retrieval process for the preservation of deteriorating library materials. The commission has also provided support for a demonstration of image processing and electronic transmission between the Library of Congress and the Avery Library of Columbia University of optically scanned deteriorating architectural materials. The National Agriculture Library has made great strides in similar preservation and distribution programs based on a system that can scan text and convert it to both digital page images and digitized ASCII code.

Replacing Microfilm

This type of effort must quickly replace the many microfilming projects now under way. The energies and funding used for these projects should be turned to creating large databases of electronically retrievable images—which are more easily and effectively stored, retrieved, and shared than microfilm. Such an image-based system, supporting journal literature access and distribution, would be a virtual national periodicals center come at last.

Even as this article has developed, the Yale University Library prepared a report, under contract with the CPA, describing a project to study the feasibility of converting large quantities of materials preserved on microfilm to digital images. The report suggests that "major contributions [have been made] to the development of imaging technology . . . . The time is right for another major step toward making digital imagery a practical library tool."[5]

Image-based systems for information sharing, such as the RLG's delightfully poetic and effective Ariel—the technological and software workstation configuration which can scan and transmit images across the Internet or other carrier—should be quickly networked throughout appropriate regions or organizations. (An information flow warning: many of these "advances" are proving to require much manual effort to retrieve and scan physical volumes.)

Replacing the Commercial Sector?

Widespread suggestions have been made for the establishment of publishing or information-distribution mechanisms in not-for-profit agencies as replacements for commercial-sector publishing. The OCLC and the American Association for the Advancement of Science, which publishes the weekly journal *Science,* are working on a joint electronic publishing venture that is expected to result in an electronic journal. And several dozen new electronic publications, such as *Postmodern Culture, New Horizons in Adult Education,* and the *Journal of the International Academy of Hospitality Research,* have begun to appear from university bases, though most are yet without formal university sponsorship.

Several hundred online library catalogs are available over the Internet, many with additional electronic tools or information sources available through campus information systems evolving from the local online catalog. The University of Southern California, for example, has added several full-text databases to its campus information system, is collaborating with the *Chronicle of Higher Education* in adding a full-text version of that journal to the USC system, and is vigorously involved with McGraw-Hill in the establishment of a print-on-demand textbook database.

Similar efforts to introduce users to electronic text-delivery capabilities through local campus online catalogs are under way from Texas to Ohio to Delaware. Each deserves to be encouraged as a means of rechanneling the traditional course of the information flow; of encouraging fresh examinations of the agencies, the currency, and the exchange points involved in the flow; and of forcing the redistribution of resources.

It will be interesting to observe the economic rebalances that begin to assert themselves in these processes, just as it will be to observe the improvements in service and information delivery that result.

Over the past few years, librarians and others who care for library collections have joined in developing a massive and successful national program for preservation. The slow fires of collection disintegration have threatened our information past. A lava flow of literature and information inflation, however, may threaten the entire future of information as we know it.

Not only is it important that libraries and scholarly publishers, along with other academic, computing, and information community colleagues, join in creative ways of breaking out of the traditional mold that holds us captive to the crisis; it may be that a major national effort must be enjoined on the access side of the information mountain just as it has been on the preservation side. Securing the information future is just a bit more important than securing the information past.

It is especially important that agencies which can be effective catalysts in addressing this issue bring their efforts together in the same manner in which they have supported the national preservation program and the prospective National Research and Education Network, or NREN (where there needs to be as much emphasis on the traffic and its load as on the highway). The CPA should, with the main aspects of a supportive infrastructure for preservation efforts in place, put even more emphasis on the "access" part of its name, in the very broadest of terms: "Providing Access to the Accumulated Human Record as Far into the Future as Possible," as its newsletter states. Support for efforts such as the Columbia–Library of Congress demonstration and those at Cornell and Yale are important, but a larger coordinated national imaging project, embracing such activities as Project Gutenberg, should be advanced.

The Council on Library Resources continues to be a powerful national catalyst for promoting new models of managing the information flow and could well be a prime mover in establishing a comprehensive, coordinated national imaging and delivery program. The Association of Research Libraries has become a stronger force in recent years in making scholars, publishers, and congressional leaders more aware of national information issues and in helping shape national policy and action. And what better purpose could the Coalition for Networked Information have beyond supporting the NREN than the reshaping of the points of tension within the information flow toward a new economy for our knowledge system?

Library schools offer still another arena where ideas can be questioned, analysis can be accomplished, and models for change constructed. And the major funding agencies, federal and private, need to have both the crisis and the opportunity of information access made as clear to them as have been the needs for support of bibliographic access and preservation in the recent past.

While the means are at hand, the solutions are not easy. While everything moves at extraordinary new speeds, the problems will not be quickly resolved. But we must begin. Bold strokes at individual and national levels can, with the technology and vision available to us, reconstruct the economics of the information flow and solve the information crisis in our time.

NOTES

1. For an excellent source of documentation on the specifics of library materials' price increases and their effects on university libraries, see Ann Okerson and Kendon Stubbs, "The Library 'Doomsday' Machine," *Publishers Weekly* 238 (February 8, 1991): 36–37.
2. By the end of 2001, Project Gutenberg had still not quite achieved its goal of converting 10,000 widely used books to electronic text.
3. Reva Basch, "Books Online: Visions, Plans, and Perspectives for Electronic Text," *Online* 15 (July 1991): 13–23.
4. Nancy Eaton, "Document Delivery and On-Demand Publishing: Implications for Reference Service," a paper presented at the General Libraries seminar "Future of Reference IV," University of Texas at Austin, February 23, 1991. Published in *College & Research Libraries News* 53, no. 8 (September 1992): 508–10+.
5. Donald J. Waters, *From Microfilm to Digital Imagery* (Washington, D.C.: Commission on Preservation and Access, 1991), 38.

5

~~~

Supping with the Devil
New Library Alliances in the Information Age

He who sups with the devil should have a long spoon.
<div align="right">—Proverb</div>

Most librarians would probably agree that the words which best characterize the major strategic mechanisms for change in libraries during the past twenty years have been "cooperation," "networking," and "resource sharing." If these powerful forces have worked to the betterment of libraries in the past, it would appear reasonable to believe that libraries will continue to turn to them to meet the problems and to grasp the opportunities of the present.

Individual libraries by themselves still cannot solve the fiscal and information crises that continue to overwhelm each of them and which so transcend the local scene. Nor can each alone make the most effective use of the new information technologies, establish reasonable standards for library applications of these technologies, and create an international information infrastructure that incorporates the best means of supporting research and scholarship while also satisfying the more modest needs of all seekers for knowledge.

Home alone is just not good for libraries. It is questionable, however, whether the specific arrangements and programs that have supported library cooperation, networking, and resource sharing in

This article was originally published in *Wilson Library Bulletin* 68 (October 1993).

the recent past will continue to be as effective at a time when technological changes shift as quickly as the sea, and when economic issues
demand that librarians recognize information for the commodity that
it is and handle it in a business-like manner. New alliances for development and business ventures in the computing and information
industries are forming regularly, and new library alliances are emerging as we advance beyond the edges of the information age.

That Old-Time Library Cooperation

National bibliographic utilities and regional library networks, established and managed on a membership basis, applied new technologies
and cooperation to achieve the improvements of the past twenty years,
marking the most progressive era of library and information services
enhancement in modern library history. Through cooperative cataloging programs, massive bibliographic databases were built that made
library materials more readily available to the user, reduced library-
processing costs, and stimulated preservation and other resource-
sharing activities. A remarkable level of bibliographic control and
information sharing was achieved on virtually a worldwide basis. These
cooperative efforts are still forcing significant organizational and
staffing changes throughout our libraries. However, like the starlight
we see after its million-light-years' journey from a star now long dead,
libraries may still be responding to influences from cooperative
systems that no longer fit the scholarly, social, economic, telecommunications, and technological times.

The infrastructural changes resulting from the alteration of long-
held organizational and processing patterns have allowed a redistribution of libraries' fiscal and human resources. This has improved
effectiveness and efficiencies, and has at least provided a minor
amount of support for other programs such as collection development.

The development of skills required for staff to meet the requirements of a new library model, not the old, has been promoted. The
changes have encouraged the establishment of virtual library management systems that are neither completely flat nor hierarchical, but
hyper-matrixed much like information itself in its hypertext form.
Libraries are benefiting from staff involvement and staff sharing across
interdepartmental lines, helping broaden the capabilities of employees and providing additional functional backup.

By way of benefit from the early network cooperative model, the old cataloging order is now seeing more paraprofessional responsibility for cataloging routines, a loosening of formerly rigid (and very costly) national standards, and a move toward machine-assisted processing which will continue to simplify and streamline the work required of people.

Nevertheless, as Carol Mandel has observed, cataloging cannot be reduced to a uniform elemental simplicity.[1] Cataloging provides an important value-added dimension to information in any format, and electronic information sources available through advanced retrieval technologies already require the application of entirely new concepts of cataloging, if not a complete reinvention of the analytical and locational processes we call cataloging. What shaped the catalog card must now more richly describe what is attainable through what Mandel calls a "catalog/window."[2]

I suspect the longer-term answer to the cataloging issue lies in another model that Mandel mentions, one in which "The finding tool can be merged with the material itself." The information object will be its own catalog entry, identifier, and mechanism for delivery.

Information available through the World Wide Web lies in a digital sea without form or evaluation, and the creation of some element of order among networked information sources requires a cataloger's touch. Some regular review, evaluation, and selection process—perhaps through a cooperative global mediator—is needed to identify those information sources that are of the most potential and enduring value to a seeker for knowledge through "catalog/window" access.

Who is going to throw out the networked information trash?

Computerized indexes are rapidly compounding ease of access to library materials on the one hand, and contributing to an interlibrary loan delivery overload on the other. Information delivery mechanisms for every format continue to be a major problem. The transfer of traditional packages of information—books and journals—is still constrained by the limitations of physical delivery mechanisms. Traditional interlibrary lending is a heavily labor-intensive, generally slow, and less than satisfactory means of information sharing. The capacity of the library community to sustain increases in typical interlibrary lending services has already surpassed a saturation point. Anyone who believes these services can be jacked by the addition of staff is not being fiscally realistic. The new computing and telecommunication technologies, however, offer hope for improved information delivery and representation based on digitization and the electronic distribution of images and text, either on disk or over a network. The interlibrary service system that emerges will be a complex of several methods of information sharing.

Where libraries and other information agencies once concentrated on the collaborative building of bibliographic databases and resource-sharing systems, like those described previously, it appears that they should now join in the cooperative building and maintenance of files of electronically imaged and digitally converted full-text information sources, and in the development of software and systems that chart a new geography of this digital information world.[3]

These data can be stored in widely distributed information servers and made available through open-system, Z39.50-compliant clients in the thousands of ubiquitous microcomputers dotting like colorful caravels the shipping lanes of a digital information sea. While conversion, storage, refreshment, and delivery of data in these files are not without significant cost, the technology which supports these functions is improving rapidly and the costs are dropping—and, most importantly, will continue to do so. This is certainly in contrast to the steeply sloped climb of the costs of traditional library materials, of interlibrary lending, and of operational support.

Some form of national and international cooperative action similar to the effort that went into the bibliographic and preservation successes of the past two decades is required. Every dollar that goes into the information system should be one that will help leverage and energize a new and healthier information world. It is especially important that the large amounts of funding and human effort going into micrographic preservation also help construct a platform for the support of electronic image exchange. Thanks to the concerns of the Commission on Preservation and Access, steps to assure this have begun.

In an encouraging introduction to the 1991–92 *Annual Report* of the commission, Patricia Battin thoughtfully explores the differences between the worlds of analog and digital preservation. She observes, "It is essential that the knowledge from the past that we preserve today meets the needs of future scholars. And in the process of preserving the past, we can make substantial strides toward the digital library framework for the future."[4]

Cooperation in the Information Age

The organization of cooperation has been in a state of uncertain renewal for the past several years. It is apparent that many institutions and resource-sharing organizations are only beginning to understand that the comprehensive collection-based library model of the recent past has been changed forever. Many libraries only recently appear to understand that they can no longer find a traditional means by which collection comprehensiveness can be maintained just as it once was. Many institutions pursue the establishment of electronic information-delivery systems on an independent basis, without adequate national collaboration or direction.

The national and regional networks at their grass roots, despite providing excellent new training programs and helpful information products, continue to apply more of the same old solutions to problems, which may have mutated beyond cure with the common elixirs. Nonetheless, cooperation in general and resource sharing in particular are still important means by which libraries can help meet rising costs, brave the new technologies, and restore a diminishing information base.

The leverage of the many has erected technical-support systems for the all that none could afford alone. However, such action in the past was something that libraries undertook chiefly with one another. For all the cooperation of the 1970s and 1980s, some libraries found they could not always work comfortably with one another or with another's network, much less with other agencies whose responsibilities were beginning to intersect those of libraries at points throughout the information flow.

Uniting in networks, whether "elitist" or populist, libraries moved toward common goals made possible by the development of the MARC format, the creation of huge granaries of bibliographic information, the development of computer-based software for the storage and retrieval of this bibliographic information, and by improvements in telecommunications—all facilitating the distribution of services built on this new framework.

Competitive tugs between these library networks led to relational difficulties among a number of libraries and library organizations as the 1970s gave way to the 1980s.[5] In the heat of competition some library groups became virtually anathema to one another. The relationship between library network competitors remains somewhat uneasy even today, as each tries to establish its own niche in the rapidly changing information scene.

At the same time, as programs were built on new technological platforms, librarians found themselves needing to develop more agreeable relationships with those new neighbors at the information frontier—computing staff, telecommunication professionals, and other electronic information experts.

Attempting to work cooperatively with computing and other technical staff who seemed ready to absorb libraries into rather frightening unlibrary-like campus agencies left librarians feeling defensive and even more contrary among themselves. After all, who besides librarians were trained to select, acquire, organize, preserve, and disseminate the information necessary to support the academic needs of students and faculty?

In fact, as some institutional administrators on college campuses surveyed the evolving systems that were bringing library and computing professionals together, the idea of appointing a senior academic officer with combined responsibility for both the library and the academic computing center became a frequently discussed, if only occasionally established, option.

Although some institutions are still attempting to make the merged arrangement work, and may be doing so effectively in certain local situations, this concept seems generally to have been wisely laid aside. Library and informational professionals, and the leadership in computing and other new technology areas, are finding other methods by which they can work together towards commonly shared development and service objectives. At my own institution, the members of a campus-wide Information Services Discussion Group, comprising a handful of upper-level administrators and hands-on managers in the library and in academic and administrative computing, keep one another apprised of strategic developments in the technological, service, fiscal, and political aspects of computing, communications, and electronic information. The development of a campus information policy is presently under discussion.

As for-profit firms began to offer an increasing array of electronic indexes and other computer-based information services, they too appeared to threaten the traditional paper-based library culture. As the old proverb had it, librarians were routinely being asked to sup with new devil after devil, and many did not—and still do not—recognize that the long electronic spoon that had helped shape the threat also offered through closer alliance the means for solution.

A meeting held at the University of California at Irvine in the fall of 1992, under the aegis of the American Council of Learned Societies and the Getty Art History Information Program, explored issues involving humanistic research and teaching in the technology revolution. William Y. Arms, of Carnegie Mellon University, was quoted as saying, "Universities are plagued by caste distinctions that inhibit teamwork. Faculty treat non-faculty colleagues with disdain, professional librarians act like a medieval guild, and computing professionals consider technical knowledge the only measure of worth."[6] He continued, "The cultural divide between the humanities and the sciences is well known, but an equally deep divide lies between scholars, librarians, and computing professionals."

Not only must one sup with old devils, but new partnerships must be built. Joint ventures can produce more effective, user-friendly indexes linked to document and information delivery systems. Joint efforts can bring better organization to the presently unbridled distribution of electronic information. Joint efforts can better construct the mechanisms for access to and evaluation of the flotsam afloat everywhere in this growing digital ocean. Libraries and the scholarly community should cooperate to develop unbundled journals, establishing systems for review, sponsorship, and imprimatur by learned societies of articles published electronically and distributed at the quick of completion. The establishment of a peer review process to support alternative publishing systems to distribute on a timelier basis the results of university-supported research and scholarship would appear to be an excellent role for the Association of American Universities (AAU) and the American Council of Learned Societies (ACLS).

The New Alliances

The full impact of the information age on society, industry, and education is only beginning to become apparent. The tectonic results are most visible through the downsizing or right-sizing of organizations ranging from libraries and universities to major corporations, through the merging of businesses and the creation of new joint efforts among them, through the military defense-conversion enterprises now being established, and through the place that information content has assumed as the international coin of progress.

The generation now entering the workplace can only contribute to society as responsible citizens and as productive members of a skilled, competitive workforce if the educational system through which they have progressed has prepared them, not just for the industrial age that is passing, but for the information age that is already creating remarkable changes, dislocations, risks, and new harmonies in the world they face. Improving the ability of this generation to use effectively the information tools that are burgeoning around them through education and training is a key responsibility that the educational community, the commercial sector, and libraries must share. Current employees who lack these skills should be provided with sufficient training to prepare them for new roles in the changing workplace.

For libraries to fulfill their long-held responsibilities as the chief stewards of the information and wisdom left by our intellectual progenitors, and whose collections and information services are the primary catalysts for the construction of new dreams and the advancement of knowledge, they must forge new alliances in this flowering information age. The word "alliance" is much more suggestive of the businesslike type of cooperation that is now developing among information organizations of various sorts than are the earlier-used appellations for networks of individual libraries working collaboratively towards common ends. Libraries are indeed closer to being shareholders these days than merely stakeholders.

A major relational shift is needed so that libraries can also join with agencies and firms in the commercial sector in new partnerships to frame the information future. Too much suspicion, competitiveness, and hostility prevail between the public and for-profit camps, despite the fact that information vendors have been using libraries as test beds and sometimes as shills for their products, and perhaps because of the fact that libraries themselves are becoming hucksters of systems and information products.

William Neikirk in a syndicated article says, "The economy is undergoing a turbulent transition to a world in which goods and services compete more for their 'information content,' which includes the sophistication of their technology and design, than on how cheaply they can be mass produced."[7]

This is the very stuff of libraries.

Neikirk adds, "A novel brand of capitalism is being born in which state and local government, universities and businesses are increasingly teaming up to form new companies and revitalize old ones."

Libraries have already reached beyond other libraries for partners in new cooperative ventures. The establishment of the National Research and Education Network through the Coalition for Networked Information (CNI) shows that all sorts of institutions are anxious to participate in forward-reaching activities. And this fresh collaboration of groups that seemed to avoid one another in the past also appears healthy—the joining of the library, academic computing, and scholarly communication communities under the CNI umbrella formed by the ARL, CAUSE, and EDUCOM.

In fact, the CNI is one of the fastest growing and most successful not-for-profit alliances ever created. Its mission is "to promote the creation of and access to information resources in networked environments in order to enrich scholarship and to enhance intellectual productivity."[8]

It is significant that the CNI is not a membership-driven organization like earlier networks, but is an organization formed by organizations and managed by them. Earlier cooperative efforts were designed so that individual libraries could share the resources and experience of each in a generally democratic fashion towards cost reduction and improvements in basic library programs. The CNI has been effectively focused on achieving more specific national networked information goals through the ideational, political, and financial weight of the many, not through the technical abilities of each.

The three organizations that joined in shaping the CNI initiative (ARL, CAUSE, and EDUCOM) formalized their relationship as the Higher Education Information Resources Alliance (HEIRAlliance), a collaborative venture that transcends the immediate interests of the memberships of each organization and is attempting to define and generate solutions to major issues facing higher education in the new information technology environment.

Similarly, the Commission on Preservation and Access, formed through multi-organizational efforts to solve a specific problem, is reaching far beyond its initial thrust of informing the scholarly community and others of the "slow fires" of destruction among our printed cultural heritage and of supporting the development of solutions to this problem. It has accepted a role that identifies preservation as the provision of continuing access to recorded knowledge as far into the future as possible. In this role, the CPA has successfully supported programs that are examining the transformation of print-based knowledge collections of the past into the digital information systems of the future.

The CPA has supported a number of important pilot projects in this area that point also towards new kinds of cooperative ventures. The collaborative efforts of Cornell University and the Xerox Corporation to validate the use of digital image technology to capture the contents of brittle books and to produce printed paper facsimiles appear to have been quite successful. A second phase of the project has been funded, this to test access over the Internet to the Cornell Digital Library and to determine the feasibility of digital-to-microfilm conversion. A contract with the University of Southern California joins that institution with Cornell and the Eastman Kodak Corporation in a project to explore the feasibility of using the Kodak Photo-CD process for preservation and access to deteriorating photographic collections. Yale University's Project Open Book has been funded for a second phase, this one with the Xerox Corporation, to devise a production-level process to convert volumes from microfilm to digital images.

The Library of Congress, for all its staid reputation, and for all its overly critical press during its recent reorganization, has become a powerful force in promoting access to multimedia informational tools through efforts like its American Memory Project. The networked availability of the information riches of the imaged documents in its remarkable exhibits of Soviet documents, Vatican archives, historical voyages, and scrolls from the Dead Sea allows a local electronic re-creation of these exhibits at any Internet site throughout the networked world. The LC must be recognized as a major partner and leader reborn that had best be fully restored to the cooperative scene, lest it pursue again a lonely vision of the library future. In its role as host to the national Cooperative Cataloging Council and other library common causes, the LC is again achieving success in supporting the full cycle of the information process: selection, acquisition, identification, organization, promotion, delivery, preservation, and other services. Like Lucius Shepard's mythological "Dragon Griaule," the Library of Congress does not sleep alone on a hill; it is the hill.

Libraries and Publishers

Above all, perhaps, librarians and publishers should sit down at a table of common purpose and join again in what has always been a necessary partnership: to publish and make available the ideas and creative work of authors. Through some strange distortion of values, publishers and libraries alike appear to have assumed their mission to be greater than that of the author, the creator. Each has developed intransigence based on the use of copyright as both a weapon and a defense that prevents the restoration of their longtime association.

Librarians believe that fair use, like charity, endureth all things. In my opinion, librarians should more vigorously acknowledge up front that publishers, like the devil, deserve their due. Fair use should be carried to the limit, and libraries should then pay for appropriate, reasonable use beyond that point.

Publishers need to overcome their fear that libraries will use any means possible to copy beyond fair use. They must try harder to understand the financial difficulties that libraries cannot control and the technological changes they must embrace. At a meeting of the American Association of Publishers (AAP) in New York in the fall of 1992, there were numerous concerns expressed about libraries' "document delivery business," which was estimated as a $60–70 million annual enterprise; about the possibility of "faculty retention of copyright"; and about congressional legislation raising "serious concerns about copyright" and a fear that the Library of Congress would soon be competing with the private sector.[9]

The tone had modified somewhat at the AAP's Professional and Scholarly Publishing (PSP) Division's annual meeting in the spring of 1993, though members alleged that "Cross-border document delivery through commercial services, or interlibrary loan . . . plays an increasing role in the erosion of journal subscriptions and sales of books to libraries."[10]

It was acknowledged that "Library funding has not kept pace with the funding of research and the increased output of scientists," and the PSP was urged to assist libraries to "get increased library funding onto the federal agenda." Tom Paul of International Thomson reportedly suggested that publishers pay more attention to the growth potential in the electronic publishing sector, and he "sees the need for strategic alliances with other information providers." Further, "the gap between research and library funding . . . [is] the biggest single problem that bedevils PSP publishers."

Earlier advice from the Council on Library Resources seemed not to have been heard: "How can publishers and libraries work together via experiments that demonstrate processes of change that are beneficial to both segments as well as to the end users?" And again, "a few well-chosen projects can begin to move us toward a more rational environment in which both information producers and information consumers are served well by libraries."[11]

One such project is TULIP (The University Licensing Program), a cooperative research project established by Elsevier and some fifteen libraries to test systems for the networked delivery and use of journals. An especially appealing project is the Red Sage Project, in which Springer-Verlag New York, AT&T Bell Labs, and the University of California at San Francisco are experimenting with the representation of complete journals on a computer screen, in bit-mapped and ASCII formats, whose "pages" can be flipped and read, and which supports the selective dissemination of information and other value-added services. In spite of these efforts, however, cultivating a more positive ongoing relationship between libraries and publishers seems to be a Sisyphean task.

Renaissance Librarians

The establishment of the National Research and Education Network (NREN) demonstrates the new interest at the federal level these days in high-performance computing, and in the establishment of information banks and electronic highways to house and carry information products—all from both public and private collaboration. The National Information Infrastructure Act of 1993 (H.R. 1757) would provide funding authorization to move towards a fully national information infrastructure with appropriate roles for both the public and private sectors. These ideas have assumed a central position in the Clinton-Gore administration's agenda.

Nothing can promote collaboration more than the allure of new government dollars. Libraries should not overlook the substantial funding opportunities available through participation in the Technology Reinvestment Project, an initiative authorized under the Defense Conversion, Reinvestment, and Transition Assistance Act of

1992. With $471 million available in 1993 and amounts that may total $10–20 billion over the next four years, the computing and library communities, businesses, and educational institutions should seize the opportunity to move a cooperative information agenda forward. As the Defense Technology Conversion Council says, "An important component of the . . . Project is providing an opportunity for various institutions to forge new relationships and engage in collaboration to their mutual advantage."

Just as political and information walls have tumbled in recent years, neither geography, nor devil, nor any other limitation should be allowed to stand between humankind and knowledge. The knowledge system of the future, containing as it will traditional collections of library materials reknit and enhanced by electronic information servers and workstations, will demand renaissance librarians and renaissance scholars alike, at willing work among the creators, distributors, and consumers of the new knowledge in the format to come.

Classes of students will share texts and work through assignment results together with their teachers in increasingly enhanced and interactive electronic modes, perhaps thousands of miles apart. Researchers will share sources, collaborate in ways still to be imagined, and produce results that are truly team efforts. Indeed, the provenance of authorship may become increasingly difficult to document. The process of cognition itself may change as new representations of information become available. Learning and scholarship will be advanced by human skills that are centuries old, as well as by machine skills developed perhaps by other machines and software written by other software.

Collaboration and resource sharing, cooperation and new alliances, partnerships of profits and not-for profits will surely help the advance of the information age. But despite the prophets who say "Good-bye, Dewey decimals" and "In lieu of librarians we will have programmers and database experts," it is still only the librarian who can effectively work that borderland between the old and the new information models.[12]

But that is another story.

NOTES

1. Carol Mandel, presentation at the Center for Research Libraries' Annual Council Meeting, Chicago, April 23, 1993 (from the author's notes).

2. Carol Mandel, "Library Catalogs in the Twenty-First Century," *ARL: A Bimonthly Newsletter* (September 9, 1992): 1–4.

3. Harold Billings, "The Bionic Library," *Library Journal* 116 (October 15, 1991): 38–42.

4. Patricia Battin, introduction to *Commission on Preservation and Access Annual Report, July 1, 1991–June 30, 1992* (Washington, D.C., 1992), 1–4. No one has worked more tirelessly than Patricia Battin in seeking means to preserve humankind's intellectual heritage. In a later time, Battin and others interested in preserving the knowledge content of various forms of the published record would come under personal attack in Nicholson Baker's distorted book, *Double Fold.* Baker correctly points out some of the oversights and failures of early attempts to develop a means to preserve the intellectual contents of libraries on a massive scale, at times unfortunately forsaking the artifact. I disapprove of his reducing the historical record to a dishonest, personal attack on Battin and others, however. Those pioneers looked to new technologies to keep alive the ideas in publications that seemed—and still are—at hazard from a host of destructive agents.

5. Harold Billings, "Governing Library Networks: The Quick and the Dead for the 1990s," *Library Journal* 114 (November 1, 1989): 49–54.

6. Beverly Watkins, "Scholars Are Urged to Collaborate in Today's 'Technology Revolution,'" *Chronicle of Higher Education* (October 28, 1992): A25.

7. William Neikirk, "The Shrinking of Corporate America," *Austin American-Statesman,* April 25, 1993, sec. D.

8. Coalition for Networked Information, "Spring 1993 Task Force Meeting: Summary Reports," various unpaginated processed documents (Washington, D.C., 1993).

9. Janice Kuta, "AAP Seminar Explores Document Delivery," *Publishers Weekly* 239 (November 30, 1992): 20–21.

10. Fred Kobrak, "PSP Meeting Concentrates on New Electronic Technologies," *Publishers Weekly* 240 (March 1, 1993): 7, 12.

11. Council on Library Resources, "New CLR Program Areas," *CLR Reports* 5 (December 1991): 6.

12. David Charbuck, "Good-bye, Dewey Decimals," *Forbes* (February 15, 1993): 204–5.

6

~~~

The Information Ark
Selection Issues in the Preservation Process

'Tis time to observe Occurrences, and let nothing remarkable escape us; The Supinity of elder days hath left so much in silence, or time hath so martyred the Records, that the most industrious heads do finde no easie work to erect a new Britannia.
—Sir Thomas Browne, *Urne-Buriall* (1658)

Those of us concerned with the preservation of information and knowledge must not forget that our mission is without journey's end. Our commitment must be that letter-headed by the Commission on Preservation and Access: "Providing Access to the Accumulated Human Record as Far into the Future as Possible." For all the successes of recent years, there are still apocalyptic and entropic forces that threaten the products of the scholarly, creative, research, and cultural processes, and that will never be completely conquered. It is also wise to acknowledge that information past and information future will be remarkably different from one another, and threats to them and processes to protect them will change as well. There has been, and will be, one constant throughout this effort. The single most important challenge in the preservation process is selection.

In the literature relating to preservation, the most perceptive and prescient commentary can be found in the introductions by Patricia

---

This article was originally published in *Wilson Library Bulletin* 68 (April 1994).

Battin, as president of the Commission on Preservation and Access, to the annual reports of the commission. In the 1992–93 report, she contends that digital technology has created "a new definition" of our concept of preservation: "Preservation is access, and access is preservation."[1] To me, this urges the inclusion of a more holistic information world than we have yet addressed in our preservation concerns.

In considering selection issues within this context, I suggest more attention be paid to a wide variety of data sources that are at access risk on the information event horizon. These include not only collections housed in libraries and archives, but new book and journal publications increasingly unpurchased for institutional collections, electronic publications and data distributed through digital information systems, and collections of books, manuscripts, and other special materials held in private hands. Other issues include selection philosophy, administration, and related library and information science education.

The Agony of Choice

Despite our many efforts, library collections reveal the increasing scars of paper disintegration and the abuse of users. Libraries continue to be diminished by their inability to maintain even a minimally acceptable level of journal subscriptions and new monographic publications. Funds for the purchase of general retrospective or replacement publications, for the purchase of manuscript and archival materials serendipitously discovered in attics or estates, and for the purchase of rare book and special collections gathered by private collectors and now come to market are simply no longer available. Insufficient resources hamper the building and retention of our libraries' collections.

There is no dark feeling quite like that of knowing our libraries are losing the high ground of collection comprehensiveness that many worked so long and hard to attain. Of knowing that many of the ideas of yesterday and today will not exist for rumination tomorrow. Or that the manuscript artifacts and digital relics that help illuminate the creative auctorial process will disappear into paper or electronic trash heaps.

It is ironic that most of the materials and information selected for preservation attention during the past few years are already located in library collections. These books, journals, and other library materials, by the very fact of their acquisition at the initiative of a bibliographer or other scholar, have already been identified as worth saving—but the reselection and reacquisition of those most deserving of a longer life, not just the effort to preserve them, is a truly immense and expensive task.

Henry Riecken, consultant to the Council on Library Resources, who has written extensively about preservation issues, acknowledges, "There are more library books and journals in need of preservation today than can possibly be saved before they crumble and disappear. Accordingly, we cannot afford to spend resources on the preservation of materials that are unimportant. Choices must be made."[2]

Riecken urges planning efforts to establish strategies to make "the hard choices as to what and how to preserve."[3] He stresses the need to bring the scholarly community to a realization that "There are neither resources nor time enough to save the total contents of the nation's libraries. Some . . . will literally disappear into dust."[4] The worst of it, Riecken says, is "the agony of choice."[5]

Librarians face policy issues regarding choice that they may well not have considered to be part of the preservation issue. They have been exposed all their careers to pictures of books housed in medieval or other early libraries that are chained, or caged, or branded. These illustrations have always seemed to invoke among librarians a reaction of perverse amusement at their information ancestors, or the feeling that these books are symbolic of restricted, not open, information access. The truth is that those wonderful, wonderful books were being protected against theft and the prospect of knowledge once lost never again available. Libraries were practicing preservational security with the technology of the time.

Libraries are torn on the horns of access versus preservation. The Library of Congress has been sharply criticized for closing its stacks. In its defense, Librarian of Congress James H. Billington cited an inventory completed a few years ago that showed some 300,000 books unaccounted for. As he pointed out, "Permitting direct access had inflicted a terrible hidden cost."[6]

However, denying easy access to information sources by students and faculty flies in the face of the scholarly process. Anything that diminishes artistic and ideational creation inhibits the growth of knowledge and the progress of humankind. In time, digitized information surrogates will make unnecessary the actual physical handling of some manuscripts or expensive printed materials, and will make possible the virtual examination by any user of such material. This will help ease the present service versus security dilemma.

Reformatting for Future Generations

Time itself constructs rare book collections around us as we work—
"Time," as Sir Thomas Browne had it, "which antiquates Antiquities,
and hath an art to make dust of all things." Collection management is
an important component of a selection activity that includes collection development, conservation, and preservation.

Materials located in library and archival collections, then, have been
the first targets of opportunity selected for a national preservation
effort. The battle to save embrittled books through micrographic and
digital scanning processes, through the gaseous infiltration of volumes
by chemical agents much like the spices that preserved the parchments
of Tutankhamen for 3,000 years, has been reasonably successful.

By March 1993, over a five-year period, the Brittle Books Program
of the National Endowment for the Humanities' Division of Preservation and Access had supported the microfilming of over 550,000
volumes in sixty-two institutions. It was anticipated that some three
million volumes would be reformatted over a twenty-year period.

In addition, during the past three years or so, other reformatting
initiatives and technical studies have begun. These include the digitization, in full-text or image, of a variety of printed materials, and the
creation and evaluation of alternative technological platforms to
transform various formats of information into another form. Various
selection processes—chiefly subject- or format-based—have been
applied to materials in library collections in determining what to
convert, and the process of selection and preservation is well under
way in this particular program. It is highly likely that the original
targets will appear somewhat modest in the next few years as methodologies change and a larger group of shape-changers join the effort.

My primary selection-for-preservation concerns at the moment
deal less with publications and information housed within collections,
but rather with those collections of archival and manuscript or early
published materials held in private hands, with those many contem-
porarily published materials that are escaping the selection nets of our
library acquisition efforts, and with that flurry of digital "publication"
in cyberspace. These latter bits of digital information and ideas leave
very fragile tracks on their cyber paths, and to this point we lack a
rational infrastructure for their control, evaluation, selection, or cataloging. The scholarly world must recognize that the acquisition of

private collections and unpurchased current publications, and the development of a review and pruning mechanism for networked digital information, are just as important in the preservation process as are those programs directed at conserving known items already in our libraries or archives.

The prospective loss of recently authored works because libraries can no longer afford to buy them, or publishers to publish them, is just as much a preservation issue as the physical loss of books printed a century ago. Can one imagine Cormac McCarthy's *All the Pretty Horses* or the novels of Toni Morrison never having had the opportunity to be read and judged for entry into the information ark that will carry today's culture on to those generations of readers who wait beyond us?

At least some publishers, faculty members, and even library staff have appeared to believe that libraries can somehow purchase more books and journals than there are funds permitting. Most libraries do understand that a current book unpurchased today may be remaindered or pulped and be unavailable tomorrow, but they remain helpless to resolve the problem. Librarians and publishers have been flailing at the same Hydra but seem to be striking only one another. Unless these parties and other scholars address in concert their common problems, there will be many more losses than are necessary.

Not too long ago, libraries and publishers worked together to establish such programs as Cataloging in Publication. They moved together to establish the standardized use of acid-free paper for printing—a collaborative success hallmarked by the symbol for infinity printed on the copyright page of most currently published academic and trade books. Libraries, the scholarly community, and publishers should share alike and share together much of the responsibility for the selection of works worthy of publication, distribution, addition to collections, evaluation, and an opportunity to live beyond their day of publication—and contribute to the means to do so. Perhaps there are better models to consider, or will be so in the near future.

At one time the author and the printer formed the publishing enterprise. The present models of scholarly communication and commercial publishing are not likely the ultimate arrangements to produce and distribute ideas and information. Edgar Allan Poe and Zane Grey both paid to have their first works published. The invisible college shows signs of metamorphosing into a new electronic scholarly publishing system. An AT&T television advertisement for hypermedia services that casts a book at a viewer from a screen confirms that other communications giants hope to establish the dimly seen vision that we might imagine today to be tomorrow's publishing scheme. One should recall, however, that advances in information, communications, and publishing processes, like motion pictures and television, rarely replace another. New formats simply add to the richness of the information sources available to us.

Funds are so relatively few, and preservation needs are so many, that careful choices must indeed be made as to where these resources should be applied. It is certain, however, that grant funding should be made as available to support the purchase of scholarly sources that still lie imperiled in private hands, at risk of every conceivable agent of destruction. Or for the purchase of currently published materials to be held in trust and made available to the many by distributed, cooperatively managed information centers of last resort, like any other type of preservation effort.

Saving One for the Many

A few years ago my institution sought federal funds to purchase a collection of Judaic archives, resting in boxes in a small house in Brazil. The collection was carried to South America like so many others in the diaspora of Judaic culture from Europe during the terrible "cleansing" of another time.

Appropriately preserved, cataloged, and made available through the national bibliographic networks, this collection would have enhanced an understanding of the collision of cultures whose reverberations still shake much of the current global political scene. It would have supported the work of scholars for years to come. There were no local institutional funds available to purchase the archive, and granting agencies thought their monies would be better spent on bibliographic access to items already safely housed in several libraries than on the acquisition of a collection for "just one institution." Moths and rust and rain forest mice have undoubtedly consumed by now that wonderful collection, and it will never receive scholarly attention. What a preservation and access paradox!

A national inventory of such resources could be developed, and cooperative efforts to develop funds to acquire, preserve, and make available this type of primary information treasure could be just as successful as joint, multi-institutional archeological excavations. Competition among libraries has conflicted for too long with the preservation of research materials.

From Print to Cyberspace

It needs to be vigorously reemphasized that future library services will continue to be based on book and journal collections. New electronic technologies will enhance and speed access to collections of printed materials, while also providing supplementary information in digital form, providing new information in formats still to be devised, and providing substitutional formats for information formerly available only in print. While the growth of paper-based collections has slowed in recent years, the total information base available to scholars has expanded as a result of resource sharing, an increase in the production of scholarly publications, and the application of advanced technologies which have enlarged and quickened the information flow.

The prodigy of the new technologies represents significant problems of a different sort. Is this digital Mississippi of information a flood of knowledge or ignorance? Who will decide what to save and how to save it, when it is becoming possible to pour terabytes of information into an unquenchable cyberspace of storage? When humankind's documentary record that is generated and distributed in digital format can be saved in virtually every textual version created, the dimensions of a selection process to identify that data worth preservation and that deserving discard reach rather incomprehensible limits.

Selection Philosophy, Administration, Education

The cultural process that persuades civilizations to retain those works of art and science that generate some deep human response in the heart of the public is in fact the selection process. Through it the choices are made that preserve and pass the intellectual products of cultures on to succeeding generations. Libraries have been major agents in this process—selection and preservation agents, but also the strongest guardians of individual rights to read and think without proscription.

Preservation follows selection in most instances, after identification of those ideas or artifacts to be preserved. In some circumstances, however, our formal preservation programs follow rather gross selection processes: all embrittled books in a collection are microfilmed, perhaps, or all volumes within a particular classification or subject area are chemically treated. This type of activity skirts the more difficult selection processes that would require a value determination on a title-by-title basis of where to spend our preservation capital. There are cost savings as well as losses in such a system, where the expense of overhead and conservation may be spent for a title not worth the choosing, even though the cost is reduced somewhat by the avoidance of the application of tighter selection principles. Choice is left to the application of principles by other agents in these grosser selection circumstances, whether that selector be time, a bibliographer, or some other scholar winnowing collections; or whether it be fashions in ideas, or the quiet abduction or ravage by a thoughtless or felonious user. The scholarly community must continue to rationalize the selection process as much as possible.

Those of us with administrative responsibilities realize that priorities must always be established and tough choices made with respect to all our services and functions. When many educators think of preservation and conservation education programs, they may think only of mending torn pages, recasing broken bindings, of book presses and glue, and possibly of microfilming and the treatment of acidic paper. With such a narrow focus, and without a broader understanding and vision of where preservation education leads, it may appear that a program that builds from basic conservation principles is more technical than academic.

To those of us who are closer to the sounds of millions of books and journals disintegrating, to the sight of frame after frame of fading motion picture film, to the realization that new monographs are being remaindered and pulped and journal subscriptions canceled because we cannot afford them, to the terrible fear that hits you when you strike a "quit" command instead of a "save" command on your computer—to those of us, conservation and preservation mean the saving of the record of our intellectual heritage for our good use today, as well as for those who wait beyond us.

Those responsible for helping to make the decisions that will preserve the human record must be able to comprehend a broad spectrum of technical processes. They must be able to understand the scholarly process and the information flow. They must understand the intricate linkages between the needs of scholars and the means to acquire, organize, preserve, and deliver information. The preservation process must be undertaken with an understanding of all these issues.

Sir Thomas Browne was able to remark, "Grave-stones tell truth scarce fourty years." We are still uncertain as to the length of life of a compact disk, yet we are committing much of our information future to digital formats in staggering numbers. We still know very little regarding this new rush of information exchange, and much serious study remains to be done.

Education, Research, and Training for a Preservation Ark

As information in electronic formats proliferates, as formats to come replace the formats of today, the complexities of saving the knowledge produced today and tomorrow, just like the record of the past, will demand even greater administrative, scholarly, and technical consideration—which is to say, a thorough understanding of the selection process. This requires the knowledge and expertise that come from a sound liberal arts education and a solid education in the principles of library and information science, supplemented by strong programs in preservation and conservation education.

There is a need for research in preservation processes and in the use of information materials. There is a need to consider the most fundamental aspects of scholarly communication so that ideas and information of true worth are not lost.

There is a need for those librarians, archivists, and conservators most knowledgeable in these matters to help educate our leaders, colleagues, students, and the public towards an understanding of the importance of conservation and preservation and of specialized education in the field of information access.

The training of preservation professionals, and the continuation of research into conservation and preservation issues, are essential to saving the record of our intellectual heritage. Without preservation we have no access. Without access we have no growth of knowledge and human progress.

Without the attention of librarians and other professional information specialists, our collections will continue to diminish, and those evolving information systems that must link both the print-based culture and the digital culture will founder.

Librarians and library schools appear clearly at risk these days, but university administrators will find over the next few years that academic programs cannot exist without them. No one else is really able to provide the intellectual linkages between the old and the new information models. Preservation education is an imperative in that responsibility.

It is possible to debate Sir Thomas Browne, and to assert that it is not sufficient to simply "observe occurrences," but to shape them; to be assertive in the selection process for preservation, to decide what ideas will be loaded one by one, or two by two, into that information ark, but acknowledge that in our ignorance and shortsightedness, we must be generous to a fault in selecting information and knowledge to preserve, so that nothing remarkable escapes us.

NOTES

The quotations in this chapter from Sir Thomas Browne's *Urne-Buriall* are from the John Carter edition (Cambridge: Cambridge University Press, 1958).

1. Patricia Battin, "Special Report: From Preservation to Access—Paradigm for the Future," in *Commission on Preservation and Access Annual Report, July 1, 1992–June 30, 1993* (Washington, D.C., 1993), 2.
2. Henry W. Riecken, "Selection for Preservation of Research Library Materials," *ACLS Newsletter,* 2nd series, 2 (winter 1990): 10.
3. Henry W. Riecken, "The Agony of Choice: Strategies for Preservation and Scholarship," in *Commission on Preservation and Access Annual Report, July 1, 1990–June 30, 1991* (Washington, D.C., 1991), 7.
4. Riecken, "Agony of Choice," 13
5. Ibid., 7
6. "Rep. Rose Holds Hearing on Security, Access to Stacks," *LC Information Bulletin* (June 28, 1993): 269.

7

~~~

The Tomorrow Librarian

Librarians and library schools are said to be very much at risk these days. The professional literature is full of predictions of the death of librarianship, and a recent surge of eschatological articles and comments in various other forums relegate libraries and library education to the dustbins of a paperless future. Given the numerous closings of library schools over the past several years, the reductions in new graduates and library staffing, and growing forays from the corporate sector into information commerce, there would appear to be generous evidence to support some of these contentions.

David Charbuck's prophetic comments in *Forbes* have been frequently quoted: "When . . . [full-text retrieval] comes, the local library as we know it all but disappears. In lieu of librarians we will have programmers and database experts."

"Good-bye, Dewey decimals," he predicts.[1]

I don't believe a word of it.

Scapegoats and Targets

In the library world itself, there has been much finger-pointing at reasons or agencies responsible for a doomsday scenario for librarianship. Some library educators have even singled out library directors

---

This article was originally published in *Wilson Library Bulletin* 69 (January 1995).

and "the profession" as culprits for many of the perceived problems of library schools.

Bert Boyce, then dean of the School of Library and Information Science at Louisiana State University, asked in his article "The Death of Library Education" "whether there will be any need for librarians in the future." If so, should their training represent a professional discipline or a trade? His answer was, yes, librarians will be needed, but "Quite simply," he contended, "it is library education, not the library, nor the need for the librarian, that is dying."[2]

The emphasis in library education should be "on the subject matter of the discipline and not on current techniques." However, absent a sufficient concern for quality, he argues, library education is perishing. High-quality education is available, but so is low-quality education, and "the cheap sack will outsell the costly sack in a free market."

Boyce concluded that the profession itself is content to let the quality of library education deteriorate, because it is easier to be mediocre than to find a way to pay for quality. "Library directors," Boyce argued, "are clearly unwilling to pay" sufficient salaries for the quality of the graduates they say they need.

I don't believe a word of it.

Every library director I know values the quality of mind, communication skills, flexibility, character, and acquired knowledge base of a new professional colleague far more than the minimal level of application expertise one would expect a recent graduate to bring to the job. And yet, skills must be mastered, and the road to a requisite knowledge base may not necessarily lead from a freestanding library school.

Library directors also continue to make every effort possible to improve their recruiting salaries for beginning librarians as well as salaries for their staff as a whole. The former is easier to accomplish, given the fewer numbers of new graduates hired, than it is to bring the salaries of an entire staff to more appropriate levels. But libraries have just as insufficient resources for salary improvements as they have to maintain adequate levels of book purchases and journal subscriptions, or to subsidize substantially the retrieval costs of electronic information sought by patrons.

Regardless of the resources available, neither a librarian nor a library educator should abjure a commitment to the pursuit of quality.

Reports of impending death for any of the three—library, librarian, library education—are premature. There are many metamorphoses and relocations under way of practitioners, educators, and the places and jurisdictions in which they function, but the ways all tend toward change, not demise. If librarianship is going through widely recognized transformations, why should not the educational programs that support the profession reflect the same forces for change? The library, the librarian, and library education will all be needed tomorrow, whether in a physical or a virtual place, or in one guise or another; and all should demand, stimulate, and produce quality in graduates, programs, and services.

Campus Vandals and Corporate Raiders

In an electronic posting on the Internet electronic discussion list JESSE, on March 14, 1994, F. William Summers, dean of the School of Library and Information Studies at Florida State University, commented, "While there are some notable exceptions, in general the relationship between LIS schools and their university libraries is not a positive one . . . One notes with dismay the almost total silence on the part of campus librarians when a library school on their campus is closed."[3]

Most members of the library profession are just as concerned about the future of library schools, and the validity of libraries and librarians in the information future, as library school deans and faculty are about library education. Librarians and their professional schools live in a very fragile academic ecosystem, and their place in the campus food chain has never been particularly strong.

Thus, Summers is accurate when he concludes, "On any campus the community of professional librarians is far too small and far too vulnerable to be isolated one from another." It is a fact, however, that educators and practitioners on any campus go about their work within different academic, administrative, financial, and political constructs, and when local institutional priorities demand some unfortunate executive decisions regarding librarianship, no amount of tears or debate will, as the *Rubáiyát* says, wipe out a word of it.

In "The Treason of the Learned: The Real Agenda of Those Who Would Destroy Libraries and Books," Michael Gorman targets other groups for some of the problems libraries are undergoing at the moment. He contends, "Libraries are under attack as never before, and none more so than academic libraries."[4]

Gorman identifies three groups of enemies of academic libraries: bureaucrats, who know little about education or libraries but who recognize that libraries cost a lot of money, and who want to reduce those costs; technocrats, who generally believe that technology can pretty much replace and improve upon traditional libraries; and technovandals, who want "to use technology to break up the culture of learning and, in a weird mixture of Nineties cybervision and Sixties radicalism, to replace that world with a howling wilderness of unstructured, unrelated gobbets of 'information' and random images in which the hapless individual wanders without direction or sense of value."

The objectives of this latter group, then, Gorman suggests, is the destruction of print-based knowledge and information industries, and, one must conclude, the construction of a bookless future without librarians or library schools. The "technovandals" would shift responsibility for the collecting, organizing, and analyzing of information from a library digital provider to an electronic end user. The services and value system of librarianship would disappear.

I don't believe a word of it. Or, at least, not most of them. The issues exist, but the groups do not. This appears to be another entry into the ubiquitous ranks of conspiracy theories and a future we will never see.

To some extent, I worry more about the concerns of frontline librarians regarding the security of their professional future than I do those of my administrative and scholarly colleagues. This frontline group has less opportunity to be heard than library directors, library school deans, faculty, and university or consortium administrators. It is also a group from which our tomorrow librarians will come.

My colleague, Dennis Dillon, one of the brightest cartographers of the new information geography, has worried in a "Future of Reference Services" forum that "libraries are going to find themselves in direct competition with billion-dollar multinational corporations."[5] Since economics will be the major determinant, he feels, of the future library, this competitive information scenario engenders real personal concern regarding future job availability in the profession.

I don't believe the competition will hurt. Rather, there needs to be a stronger synergism developed between the not-for-profit and commercial sectors based on both competition and cooperation. For years I have echoed colleagues who insist that if librarians don't take charge of new information services, others will. Well, perhaps if others can do it better, they should. Librarians should be eager to link the user and the most effective information provider, regardless of who it is. That is the higher business that we are about.

A Place in the Information Future

The role of librarians should, contrary to the more negative references already discussed, become increasingly important as scholarly communication continues to undergo at least some degree of transformation, and as the information flow continues to surge and becomes increasingly more complex. Despite any present appearances, I am convinced that academic leaders, computing professionals, and information specialists in general are going to find that there is a critical need for libraries, librarians, and library education in coming years.

The only direction that librarians and library educators should be pointing fingers these days is forward.

There is nothing we can learn from the future except by talking about it. The future is never the same as any of our predictions. Extrapolations from current events never quite arrive where we think they will. In order to understand the place of librarians in the information future, it is necessary to look just a bit at their place in the past.

The profession has never been particularly successful at self-promotion. Boyce is correct when he says that librarianship is a profession "continually uneasy with its image." In my view, hundreds of people-years have been wasted, for instance, trying to secure "faculty status" for librarians employed in academic institutions. This effort could be much better spent securing respect for the profession's members by promoting the singular contributions they make to the knowledge world as librarians. A profession that does not respect itself is not likely to be respected by others.

Despite the noise from many quarters these days, there has long been a national information infrastructure. It is called libraries. But the failure of the library profession to assert the very special and important role that its members have played in creating and maintaining this long-extant infrastructure—as librarians, and not some other breed of educational or information cat—has helped leave them without the full stature they should command. Because librarianship is a service profession, librarians working in some areas suffer somewhat from client expectations and preconceptions of them. While librarians are generally looked up to in public libraries, and regarded as professional equals among research colleagues in special libraries, they are generally not as strongly respected in academic institutions where faculty are kings. This accounts for some of the compulsive concern over the issues of faculty status by librarians in academic environments.

Another problem is that the writ of librarianship is too insular. Thank goodness for those distinguished colleagues in librarianship who have been successful in penetrating the pages of the *Chronicle of Higher Education,* the *New York Times,* and other mainstream publications with news of the profession's relevance to the needs of the day. As for publications in the field, however, the culture of librarianship is more appropriately defined in general library publications such as *Library Journal* and the *Wilson Library Bulletin,* where it can reach the broader heartland of the profession and a more general readership, than it is in many refereed publications where library specialists appear to speak only in tongues, and only to others in their field.

There comes a time when foolishness must be challenged. It is not prophecy, only common sense in the workplace of ideas, that tells us that books and a paper-based culture will be as much in our future as they have been in the past. The traditional library system will continue as closely intertwined—metaphorically speaking—with the new information technologies as the oak and linden that were Ovid's metamorphosed Baucis and Philemon.

Only the librarian has the ability to manage the traditional library system as well as the evolving bionic library in which the traditional organic enterprise is extended by and merged with the new. The librarian is educated and trained to deal with the selection, acquisition, organization, service, preservation, and training activities that are required in the print-on-paper information model as well as the digital one. Many librarians have become especially quick studies in the new technologies, without losing their feel for the old.

On the other hand, those computing and other information professionals, who are quite important to the digital platform on which electronic information flows, have had no reason or means to learn how knowledge seekers are likely to approach this fresh mixture of the old and the new systems to find the information they need. Neither are these specialists likely to learn the culture, methodologies, or management requirements of the traditional information system. Establish a rational, comprehensive information-selection program? Order a book or journal? Catalog and classify it? Process, house, service, preserve it? Only the librarian.

Select for users a new, valuable source from the host of data on the Internet, much of it only loosely describable as "information"? Attach descriptors and access and retrieval pointers? House the system; provide a menu and interface that information seekers will understand; and train users in the skills required to make effective use of these new capabilities? Surely the librarian.

One must caution, however, that this is—to borrow a phrase that has been used to define that initial bite of time at the birth of the infant cosmos—merely the first "God's second" in the Big Bang of the information age. Most of the issues, and most of the obstacles and opportunities, are still to be encountered and defined. The most exciting event yet in this new age has only recently occurred. Hypertext markup languages are now being used to tag much of the information being cast into cyberspace. This application of code to the fundamental topical and auctorial particles in an information object on the World Wide Web, that distributed hypermedia system of the Internet, simplifies and enhances information browsing, identification, and retrieval. The result is the first truly hypertextual means for information management in multiple formats, and in multiple selected scales of dimension and content, irrespective of where that information is located in the world.

Librarians and the Electronic Word

One of the most significant contributions that Richard Lanham makes in his landmark book *The Electronic Word* is to identify the importance of training and the value of dynamic information scaling in the delivery of information from a digital base.[6] An example of scaling is the selection of, or bringing to an appropriate magnitude, information objects for easy understanding and most effective use. This could amount to the reduction by a scholar of an electronic text to its most significant sentence, or the construction of customized textbooks built of links to widely distributed information sources. It could include the choice of font and size for the display of information content, and could include (as described by Lanham) the use of performative signs, "tonal colorizors," and a mix of text, sound, and image to enrich a message.

The addition of "emoticons" to e-mail conversation is an example of attempts to provide additional meaning and depth to electronic rhetoric or to an electronic information object.

It is interesting that these points which Lanham mentions—training and scaling—both speak to the importance of considering the human capacity to learn new skills and to grasp content and concept in an arena where time, speed, distance, and dimension are no longer confined by human limitations of comprehension. It must also be recognized that cognitive processes or emotional response in megabauds may not necessarily follow previous reactions to signs, signals, or other messages in a slower dimension.

These points also speak to the most important role and responsibility that librarians have always held in the information process: selection. That is, understanding how knowledge sources are created and organized, deciding in collaboration with other scholars which sources most deserve attention and preservation, and grasping the means to bring the right information, and the right amount of information, together with the user.

Richard Lanham understands this. "The library world feels *depaysé* today, and rightly so. Both of its physical entities, the buildings and the books they contain, can no longer form the basis for planning. . . . Librarians of electronic information . . . must consciously construct human attention-structures rather than assemble a collection of books according to commonly accepted rules. They have, perhaps unwillingly, found themselves transported from the ancillary margin of the human sciences to their center."

It is vital, Lanham says, if students are to be properly served by the education they should receive, for conversation to begin throughout academe regarding the information structure of the future. Where should this conversation most naturally take place, he asks? "The library or library school," he answers. Validation of the present centrality of these and other agencies does not deter Lanham from forecasting changes throughout the educational paradigm: "We're going to need a new administrative structure, a new 'informational structure' instead of a 'library,' and a new lower division with a new curriculum . . . the arts and sciences . . . converging on a common 'science of complex systems.'"[7]

Information Democracy and Anarchy

It appears to me that the new information technology is itself helping to circumscribe knowledge within this "common 'science of complex systems.'" Information access and distribution are also becoming, for both better and worse, incorrigibly democratized. There is much to be said for the avoidance of an information caste system. Demographics suggest how much at mercy society will be to the plague of illiteracy unless those of us at every level of educational responsibility work to mitigate this problem. But information is not all created equal. It is almost frightening to realize that anyone with appropriate access to the Internet, with software that is free and easily available, and with a minimal level of microcomputing power, can become a publisher to the world. Perhaps more positively, even an elementary schoolchild can construct a near-limitless personal electronic library simply by identifying and saving links to literally inconceivable amounts and types of information available from around the globe.

The information horses have been unloosed from their barns or corrals, the doors and gates all ajar, and it is difficult to see how these free-running mavericks can ever be reined in at all. Librarians can only clutch at them, tag them with identifiers when possible, and construct signposts and navigational tools to track this information at bay. Standards must be devised to help better control, if we can, the information to come.

The information world, now wild with its riders and rich in its unstructured wonders, will require the attention of architects and planners, builders, guides, computing and telecommunication specialists, engineers, legal experts, environmentalists, safety and security officers, and information specialists if it is to be turned from a wilderness into the rational, near-limitless knowledge structure that is possible.

A Role for the Educator and Academy

As there will for the librarian, there will be a role for the library and information educator in this world, although the sign they post above their door may change. Conceivably, they and their tasks may be absorbed into other schools or academic partitions on campus. The barber gave up chirurgy, the leech, and health care in general, and the world is better for it, but medical practice and medical training continue.

I have the strong feeling that library education will be reborn in those institutions in which schools have died, but as components of new educational programs wherein communication, computing, education, and other elements of the liberal and natural arts and sciences are brought together in more holistic curricula.

Regardless of the complexity of the cultural, technical, and fiscal environment surrounding information services, there is no great mystery to successful library education. Recruit bright students with a service interest and an inquiring mind, and engage and challenge them with a gifted faculty.

Insist on the inclusion of research projects and significant writing components in library educational programs. Reinstate a thesis requirement. Like medicine and law and engineering, librarianship is an applied profession as well as one based on a strong subject discipline, and library education should not be shamed for paying attention in syllabus, research, and publication to precept and practice. The profession should demand accreditation and certification—and recertification, especially as tides of change drawn by a fulling technological moon overrun our capacity for their assimilation. These changes demand fresh training and continuing education.

Despite strong support from library associations in areas of trade and social responsibility, an academic apparatus for the profession has never been fully secured. There has been no agreement reached on standards or baselines of education or knowledge to require. There is no academy. Librarians should recognize and bestow attention on those in their profession who bring distinction to the field. Fellowship in an appropriate academy could help accomplish this, and could also leverage the knowledge and experience of such a community of information experts and scholars towards the advancement of librarianship and learning.

Shaping an Information Renaissance

Just as the librarians of today are shaping the library of tomorrow, the librarians of tomorrow are being shaped today. Knowledgeable in library and information science, technologically informed, educated broadly in the basic precepts of art and humane concern, dedicated to public service, willing to be leaders and to take risks in shaping the future information society—in whatever other dimension and form it comes—the librarians of the future, like the best librarians of yesterday and today, should be conceived in the truest of renaissance traditions.

David Hoekema, academic dean and professor of philosophy at Calvin College, speaking at a symposium on scholarly publishing on electronic networks, summarized the frequently stated reasons why librarians and publishers will be unnecessary in an electronic information future, and then blew the arguments away. "We will always need interpreters, evaluators, and guides," he said; "even when the whole Western and Eastern cultural patrimony has been mounted in a digital chip . . . the need for explanation, interpretation, and conversation will remain, and it will not be met by machines."[8]

A place for librarians in the information future? Believe it.

NOTES

1. David Charbuck, "Good-bye, Dewey Decimals," *Forbes* (February 15, 1993): 204–5.
2. Bert Boyce, "The Death of Library Education," *American Libraries* 25 (March 1994): 257–59.
3. F. William Summers, posting on the electronic discussion list JESSE, JESSE@arizvm1.ccit.arizona.edu, March 14, 1994.
4. Michael Gorman, "The Treason of the Learned: The Real Agenda of Those Who Would Destroy Libraries and Books," *Library Journal* 119 (February 15, 1994): 130–31.
5. Dennis Dillon, "The Future of Reference IV: Response," *College & Research Libraries News* 53, no. 8 (September 1992): 513–14.
6. Richard Lanham, *The Electronic Word: Democracy, Technology, and the Arts* (Chicago: University of Chicago Press, 1993), 134–35.
7. Lanham, *Electronic Word*, 271.
8. David Hoekema, "Quotable: 'In the Electronic Age, the New University Library Can Be Ten Times Larger on the Inside Than It Is on the Outside,'" *Chronicle of Higher Education* (January 19, 1994): B5.

8

~~~

Library Collections and Distance Information

New Models of Collection Development for the Twenty-First Century

A discussion of library collections, distance information, and emergent models of collection development by which information resources will be managed in the new century can be highlighted by several unarguable trends.

> If there is anyone who believes print-on-paper is dying, they have not been reading publishing statistics.

> The ability of libraries to maintain acquisitions programs that keep up with the ongoing pace of paper-based publishing continues to diminish.

> As libraries continue to constrict their purchases towards their most basic needs, conventional wisdom would suggest that library collections are all beginning to look alike.

Research by Anna Perrault confirms this increasing homogeneity of academic library acquisitions and collections.[1] She notes that her findings support the Mellon report that suggests a "narrowing" of access to scholarly information, a concern that research libraries will look "more and more alike over time," and a resulting "decline in the richness of collections overall, not merely a decline in the range of holdings of any one library."[2]

This article was originally published in *Journal of Library Administration* 24, no. 1/2 (1996).

At the same time that print-on-paper publishing flourishes, the growth of distance information continues at an exponential pace. By this is meant the expansion of interlibrary services in all their variations, and document delivery in its many manifestations, as well as the creation and distribution of information objects coruscating from a digital forge.

A major task for libraries in coming years will be the addition to their collections of appropriate books and journals in paper-based format, the management of an increasing proportion of information that will become available in digital form, and the communal gathering of these information streams into a common pool for the retrieval of information.

Libraries must modify and update collection development policies and procedures to recognize that the local collection will evolve into one enhanced and extended by digital technologies and electronic information sources. Policies for managing—and sharing—national and global megacollections will emerge from the construction of cooperative programs on a scale that far transcends concerns for building the local collection.

Librarians should not be surprised that policies will be, and indeed, are already being established by those governing bodies that fund libraries to move them towards collection development practices that may conflict with what libraries have always presumed would be local or cooperative collection development decisions.

It is important that new models of collection development emerge to equip libraries, and the larger library and information community, for the responsibilities they will bear for access to all forms of information in the future.

This chapter touches briefly on issues where library collections and distance information come together on a policy level and how these issues will shape the future.

Characteristics of the New Information Environment

Let me briefly describe what I believe to be some of the characteristics of the new information environment. The changing nature of information is providing a dramatic impetus towards a reconsideration of issues that have always been basic to collection development. Both artifactual and digital information must be selected, organized, preserved, and delivered from physical collections and electronic repositories. Both analog and digital formats will be delivered locally or to distant locations by carriers appropriate to the format.

Wm. A. Wulf of the University of Virginia—in a wonderful article entitled "Warning: Information Technology Will Transform the University"—describes the changing nature of universities and libraries: "Instead of a hoarder of containers, the library must either become the facilitator of retrieval and dissemination or be relegated to the role of a museum. If we project far enough into the future, it's not clear whether there is a distinction between the library and the book."[3]

"The technology of the bibliographic citation," he continues, "pales by comparison with the hypertextual link: the ability to gain immediate access to the full referenced source and hence to browse through the context of the reference. It will take a long time to build the web and especially to incorporate the paper legacy, but the value of a seamless mesh will doom the discrete isolated volume."

Perhaps the greatest challenge in managing this wealth of collections and interwebbed information will be to find a means to merge the information sources—and the results of searching these sources—in order to provide the content that satisfies the information seeker whether it be textual information, hypertext, raw data, response-invoking semiotics such as art or music, or that grander thing that we call knowledge, whatever it may be.

The answer to this challenge will represent a resolution of economic, technological, ideational, and philosophical matters that will transform the information environment. In order to better understand that information scene, and the collection policies required to shape it, it might be well to consider some of its physical and temporal characteristics.

Time and distance will remain in the genetic structure of the print-on-paper model. Distance information carried by a stream of digital pulses is characterized by transmutability, manipulability, and a dangerous fragility. We do not yet really understand how to secure the permanent retention of such information or how to establish policies to guarantee an appropriate assignment of responsibility for its preservation.

Distance and location are of little moment to any format until the information is required. Geography is virtually negligible in the digital information world. It may not yet be the case that distance is dead, but it is certainly dying. Time, on the other hand, is very much an issue in the currentness of some content, how quickly it can be accessed, and as a condition of the mind that considers it.

Selection will continue to be the most important issue in the total process of information service. Identification of prospective scholarly resources has become simpler in many regards as bibliographic and indexing tools have improved. But selection will become more complicated as the information world itself continues to expand and as information objects grow increasingly more varied and complex.

Delivery will remain the most difficult problem for paper-based services. While distance—as noted above—is becoming virtually a non-issue in many areas of library service, it continues to be a significant barrier in others. As distance information becomes more routine—that is, as libraries rely increasingly on remote access as well as on the collections at hand—a new set of collection-building consternations will be confronted at every level of decision-making in the acquisitions process. These must be treated in library collection policies.

One of the major problems that must be addressed in the new information environment will be an appropriate choice for what will be the chief characteristic of the information object. Will it be print or will it be digital? Will it be both?

Will the digital version provide for such a richer mixture of content, of information searching and retrieval capabilities, of extended information linking and expansion of knowledge availability, that a paper version will be redundant and an unnecessary expense? Or will a paper copy represent a necessity for any one of a number of quite justifiable reasons—ease of use for content access, convenience as a mobile information unit, as a useful backup, or as a warm and fuzzy security blanket for the intellectual child in each of us?

This issue is not as simple as deciding whether to acquire a title in one format or another; whether to bind it or not; whether to discard it after a period of time when it was useful in a physical format regardless of whether a digital version exists or not; or deciding that the title has significance because of its format, quality of construction, or artifactual significance. The issue should be considered more holistically in terms of defining what the total requirements are for effective, efficient access to knowledge sources, whether on a title-by-title basis, on an object-by-object basis, or a construct-by-construct basis, within the organic information world.

What are the fiscal issues involved in these choices?

Collection development policies must include such considerations as these as they are modified to fit the circumstances of this strange and wonderful new world in which the information object itself may well be a compound of multimedia content, of both client and server software, and of self-referential cataloging data.

What are some of the other special issues and challenges that will affect collection development at that borderline of dynamic tension where the physical library collection and the digital world of compound information converge, separate, augment one another, and do battle?

First of all, libraries can be absolutely secure in their knowledge that library services will be required in the information future. Librarians will continue to build value for systems that connect information and its prospective users. Librarians will be the tool-shapers and the information guides, hunters and fishers in this new information ecology. Many will continue their work in those locations we have called libraries.

Anyone who enters an enormous warehouse of books, or a vast star space of digital knowledge that has not been thoroughly organized, will quickly have to seek a librarian to achieve any major degree of success in an information search. A library as a repository for physical collections, as a central bank of subject and information-retrieval expertise, as a station from which information missions depart, will be just as important in the information future as it has been in the information past.

On a very practical basis, libraries must negotiate much of the complex contractual web that determines which digital information a user has access to. Individuals have been able to buy books and subscribe to journals. Without some affiliation with libraries, how will individuals be able to gain access to certain electronic information that requires payment at the door, and which may not be available through a commercial information service, or available only at greater expense from a non-library source? The library as a cost-center middleman, using economies of scale in its payment for information access, and in chasing the dream of making information as freely available as possible, will continue in a digital world as in print. Libraries will impose more cost-recovery charges for information access than in the past, but it appears certain that the cost per information-unit delivered will decline.

Librarians will be indispensable in the development of collection development policies whether at the local level, at the cooperatively managed megacollection level, or within a reshaped information-management framework driven by those who control the institutional funding that dictates what libraries will collect and how they will share resources with one another.

The Establishment of Collection Development Policies

Twenty-five years ago most of our libraries were just beginning to establish collection development policies to assist in the management of their acquisition programs. Over the years these policies have been massaged, revised, perhaps even laid aside and forgotten as the quickening of research has produced more information for printed library materials, and as flat or reduced budgets have negated the best-laid plans for acquisition programs.

For the most part, those collection policies initiated in the 1970s included selection criteria regarding the academic and research interests to be supported, the scope and level of intensity at which these subjects would be acquired, and information regarding the language, publication date, and the formats appropriate for acquisition.

With the advent of expanded cooperative resource-sharing programs in the 1980s, the application of policies based on organizational agreements and national perspectives grew more intensive. These programs utilized such mechanisms as the National Shelf List Measurement Project, the RLG Conspectus, and other descriptive and analytical methodologies that were established among institutions involved in library networking cooperatives in order to rationalize collection-building responsibilities among the participants.

Collection policies, of course, had moved on to include matters relating to duplication, disposition, disaster plans, and preservation.

While granting the continuing importance of these long-standing guidelines for the development of collections appropriate to local institutional needs, or for collections joined to one another symbiotically through resource-sharing agreements, the development of the digital library begs the introduction of entirely new considerations into collection-development policy statements as libraries move into the twenty-first century.

New factors—the rapidly increasing availability of network-accessible information resources, the incorporation of digitization into numerous information activities, and the concept of managed information—have not surprisingly started to emerge as issues to be incorporated into selection policies.

In the 1995 edition of her useful textbook on collection development, the late Elizabeth Futas noted that some areas of collection development discussion "have not yet appeared in any discernible number of policies. Among these areas are the collecting and archiving of electronic journals, the Internet and its relationship to collection building, cooperative efforts in collection development and preservation of materials. Why these areas have yet to show up is somewhat perplexing since the library profession is certainly concerned about their impact on collection growth and development."[4]

Happily, these issues are now beginning to receive attention in the literature. The so-called mainstreaming of the selection of Internet resources into the collection development process has been extremely well introduced in an article by Samuel Demas, Peter McDonald, and Gregory Lawrence of Cornell University, growing out of earlier work by Demas.[5]

"We believe," they say, "it is time for collection development librarians to focus intensively on the processes of collection development as applied to networked and other electronic resources." Beyond that, as they point out, "Applying the principles of selection to Internet-accessible resources is but one part of a larger challenge: learning how to select among a wide variety of potential access mechanisms."

The recognition that the same information resources may be available in print, microform, CD-ROM, locally mounted magnetic tape files, or in digital representations via various retrieval tools on the Internet, is still just a beginning at determining how best to relate this multiplicity of resources to one another. The knowledge seeker must be able to find the content being sought whether it is in a local or remote collection and regardless of the digital format in which it is wrapped.

Each of our institutions will be exploring the addition of a new vocabulary to our collection development policies. These policies will describe the intention at the local level to deal with the mix of physical and digital resources that will be "acquired," but libraries will be looking increasingly at other issues still to be addressed in collection development policy for the twenty-first century's information environment. These issues will exist at a macro level reflecting larger institutional, state, and national policy issues rather than just the typical local collection orientation.

"Historically a university has been a place," writes Wm. Wulf. Scholars gathered where they could be safe, where there were other scholars with whom to converse, where there was access to scholarly materials, and in contemporary times, to scientific instruments and library collections. "Where the scholars assembled, the students followed," Wulf says.

He cites John Cardinal Newman's nineteenth-century essays on the university in which Newman said that if he had to describe what a university was, he would draw his answer from its ancient designation as a *stadium generale:* "This description implies the assemblage of strangers from all parts in one spot."

In cyberspace all roads lead to a digital Rome. Indeed, any road can lead anywhere and everywhere. No one need be a stranger to any place, and virtual assemblages at the desktop will be common, whether by digital access or by interactive conferencing.

Wulf continues: "With powerful ubiquitous computing and networking, I believe that each of the university's functions can be distributed in space, and possibly in time. Remote scholarship is the direct analog of telecommuting in the business world, and every bit as appealing."

It is widely suggested that computing and networking provide for a learner-centered environment rather than the traditional teacher-centered environment that has been a characteristic of the university as place. Every element of the scholarly process—teacher, student, library collection—can be centric and coincidental in the digital environment.

Toward Managed Information

It is apparent that there is a growing trend at all levels of education to consider carefully what the new technologies can do to help distribute the scholarly process, not because of the immediately perceived virtues of how technology can improve the system, but rather because of fiscal, demographic, and social pressures.

Fiscal constrictions in higher education are certainly urging a distributed responsibility among educational institutions for the provision of support for distance education and for lifelong learning. Teachers and students both must share their scholarly experience in the same company as the informational materials—the library collections—that must be readily available to them. Distance information will be a fundamental resource for distance learning. It is small wonder that there is such a strong swell of interest in digital libraries.

The forces at work at the macro level that will surely promote easy digital access to information of all kinds may well relegate local collection development policies to a secondary status. These overriding forces will at once affect local acquisitions programs as well as the resource-sharing activities through which libraries will increasingly provide access to information based on trans-institutional policies and directives.

It is clear that libraries are being steered by their funding bodies towards managed information programs, and local information-acquisitions programs and collection development policies will increasingly reveal the influences of this pressure. This tactic is not one to necessarily criticize, but it is one that should be more widely understood if libraries are to take advantage of the many opportunities it may present. Librarians should not simply be made to feel suffocated by the application of control beyond levels that they are familiar with. Any new funding or resource-sharing strategy should be considered for its potential benefits.

Collection development policies themselves have been the very instruments by which libraries have attempted to manage their local acquisition programs and collections, but this type of management has been self-imposed and is not the kind of control described above.

While not desiring to overdo an analogy with health care, it is the case that both information and health care share a number of similarities. Both are essential to the public good. Both health care and information services face substantial increases in costs that simply cannot be sustained through ordinary budget growth. Technology has been a major benefit in shaping and improving both services, but it has also helped boost costs. Both health care and information services have experienced major increases in service demands, and their attempts to manage the increased demands and costs have some striking similarities.

Movement towards managed information has been just as sure as the move towards managed health care. Library funding entities have recognized that there is no way to keep up with the levels of service demands and the rise in costs without the application of management principles to control costs by urging libraries into arrangements that take more advantage of leveraged resources. These arrangements include consortial information purchases and more centralized coordination of what has been a very decentralized system of information acquisitions. Rather than providing additional funding to individual institutions for the acquisition of multiple copies of an information object to be located at duplicative sites, funding bodies are pooling limited dollars to promote the acquisition of collections and information services to be shared from central servers among the various participants in resource-sharing programs.

In order to effectuate this policy, information management organizations have been established among libraries just like their health management counterparts have been established in health services.

The press of libraries into resource-sharing programs has been both subtle and overt. Where cooperation was once a choice that was left pretty much up to individual libraries, the new patterns that are emerging find multi-institutional funding bodies pushing libraries into arrangements for sharing local collections and access programs. This distributes the cost of information acquisition, management, and delivery activities, while also improving the range and depth of information acquired.

While local institutions and libraries may still choose whether to participate or not in some of these extended resource-sharing programs, they will get special funding or benefits from other incentives that are being made available only if they buy into centrally managed information programs.

There are several examples of the application of this developing strategy. On a national level, the establishment of the AAU/ARL foreign acquisitions programs is an example that can be cited as a "soft" model of managed information.

In this model—encouraged by university presidents, the ARL, and foundation funding—libraries assume responsibility for acquiring parts of the larger information universe while delegating the procurement of other pieces of that universe of knowledge to others. This represents a much larger commitment on a national basis than any since the days of the Farmington Plan, the National Program for Acquisitions and Cataloging, the Public Law 480 Program, and the Latin

American Cooperative Acquisitions Program. Some of these now-defunct programs were aimed at increasing duplicative holdings on an institution-by-institution basis, rather than simply ensuring that a copy would be acquired, cataloged, and preserved for the many to share. Contemporary commitments to resource sharing are being encouraged at the institutional level, at a national organizational level, and at a funding level rather than being generated most specifically at the library level.

Similarly, other library organizations—on a regional, system, or state level—are being pushed towards managed information programs. In Texas, the TexShare library information-sharing program was developed under the auspices of the Texas Council of State University Librarians. The state legislature funded it at modest but helpful levels. Those funds were initially deeded to and managed by the Texas Higher Education Coordinating Board. In order to receive the most direct benefit of this funding, libraries were asked to sign an agreement that they would participate in several specified statewide programs before they became eligible to receive funding or services being made available through the TexShare program. Recent legislation has established TexShare as a program of the Texas State Library, and state funding was increased to a level that ensured a modicum of access to digital information for hundreds of libraries in the state.

These funds are indeed being leveraged to the advantage of the participants in the program. The costs of information delivery services have been reduced while the amount of information available to the participants has been dramatically increased, but libraries have to give up a certain degree of independence in order to benefit from the managed information program.

A similar arrangement has been established among members of the University of Texas System libraries, whereby the fifteen academic and medical libraries in the UT System utilize both local funds and funds made available from central System resources to participate in mutually agreed to, managed information-service programs. It is increasingly more difficult for an institution to choose not to move its local library funding towards supporting commonly agreed to, shared programs if it wishes to gain any advantage from the seed funding provided by the central UT System source. These are not simply cooperative programs; they are efforts aimed at tightly managed coordinated activities.

Managed information programs that incorporate selection, budgeting, and fund allocation of network resources do not fit well with our existing models based on the $50 book or the $100 journal. The resources are more costly, the decisions are more complex. Are the days of the lone bibliographer or scholar making decisions on their own for the megacollections as numbered as the lone library making decisions on its own? Networking strains our organizational models and precepts, and obsolescent models and policies must give way to ones that best fit the new paradigm.

While a comprehensive survey is needed to fully assess the degree to which managed information-sharing programs are being established on a national basis, a survey by the *Chronicle of Higher Education* reported that "Statewide efforts already exist in Alabama, Georgia, Illinois, Louisiana, Ohio, Virginia, and Texas, while interstate groups have been formed among Big Ten research universities and among small liberal-arts colleges."[6]

This description of managed information services will likely find a great deal of resonance among state-supported institutions participating in these programs, while private institutions may not feel as much top-down pressure for such consortial participation as do public ones.

Given that information management organizations are already influencing the directions in which we acquire materials for our local collections as well as those we share with one another, one can envision the application of still other management policies being added as riders to funding authorizations. For example, many libraries in the course of the establishment of resource-sharing programs have said: "You collect this, and I will collect that, and we will share those collections."

Might it not be a next logical step for a coordinating body to say to those libraries in a state or university system: "All of you institutions offering graduate programs in biotechnology acquire one copy of a monograph and share it; all of you offering similar academic degree programs share in the cost of a subscription or an access license to digital information, and establish a physical or electronic carrier to distribute that information among yourselves."

In other words, do not just segregate collection responsibilities by institutional specialization, but aggregate institutionally by discipline offered and establish collection policies to reflect this practice. Never mind that the divisions of knowledge are inherently artificial, and contrary to the growth of interdisciplinary study and compound information. It should also be obvious that the establishment of standards and commonly agreed to collection and educational protocols in such an environment will be extremely difficult, but must be accomplished.

"And, oh, by the way," that coordinating body might say, "you get only one professor to share among you in teaching this discipline and in directing research."

Distance learning has been the hottest game in town and gown. It is in every library's best interest to ensure that policy makers understand that where distance learning goes it will require distance information as her handmaiden.

A New Infrastructure

In summary, contemporary collection-development policies must continue to be updated to reflect the actual practices and changes in the traditional building of local collections. They must also reflect the decisions that have been made to share collections through cooperative resource-sharing agreements, or reflect the growing trans-consortial pressure of coordinating bodies or funding agencies towards managed information and instructional programs.

Collection policies must recognize the evolving relationships between physical and digital information sources and the creation of truly new multimedia or compound information objects that include text, graphics, sound, video, and multidimensional animation—hyperlinked on a global basis.

The twenty-first century's system of information services and scholarship will be built on a new infrastructure that will be defined in every library's collection development policies. The elements included will be local acquisitions policy, collaborative agreements, managed information programs, networked collections and digital information, appropriate attention to copyright and intellectual property rights, cost recovery-based services, and—if this structure is to stand—an economic framework unlike anything that presently exists.

Both library collections and distance information will be moving together towards digital center stage as this process unfolds in the years ahead.

NOTES

1. Anna H. Perrault, "Study Confirms Increased Homogeneity in Academic Library Acquisitions," *ARL: A Bimonthly Newsletter of Research Library Issues and Actions* 189 (May 1995): 5.

2. Anthony M. Cummings et al., *University Libraries and Scholarly Communication: A Study Prepared for the Andrew W. Mellon Foundation* (Washington, D.C.: Association of Research Libraries for the Andrew W. Mellon Foundation, 1992), 3.

3. Wm. A. Wulf, "Warning: Information Technology Will Transform the University," *Issues in Science and Technology* 11 (summer 1995): 46–52.

4. Elizabeth Futas, ed., *Collection Development Policies and Procedures,* 3rd ed. (Phoenix: Oryx, 1995).

5. Samuel Demas, Peter McDonald, and Gregory Lawrence, "The Internet and Collection Development: Mainstreaming Selection of Internet Resources," *Library Resources & Technical Services* 39 (July 1995): 275–90.

6. Thomas J. DeLoughry, "Purchasing Power: Cost-Sharing Efforts Help College Libraries Finance Electronic Acquisitions," *Chronicle of Higher Education* (February 9, 1996): A21–22.

9

~~~

Libraries, Language, and Change
Defining the Information Present

It is true that the most ancient men, the first librarians, made use of a language quite different from the one we speak today.
—Jorge Luis Borges, "The Library of Babel"

What we call things affects how well we understand them. Until things are widely named and defined they resist broad study and common understanding, the El Niño meteorological effect being a case in point. The need for fresh library naming and definition is particularly important during this time of paradigmatic change. Librarians have struggled to create more contemporary metaphors for libraries in attempting to clarify what they are, or what they may become, during this metamorphosis—"digital library" being an excellent example. But a vocabulary for major concepts of change has not had the same attention.

A few years ago (see chapter 2, "Magic and Hypersystems"), I attempted to compare the knowledge systems of the sixteenth century with those of the present, suggesting that there was an opportunity for a new orderliness in libraries that could best be understood by comparing the image-based, magic memory systems of those earlier information seekers with modern computing and contemporary information systems.[1]

This article was originally published in *College & Research Libraries News* 59, no. 3 (May 1998).

One wanted, it was affirmed, to employ fresh language and images as magical as any of the sixteenth century in attempting to find new order in the structure and complexity of the natural world, to bring new dimensions to the sciences we know.

More recently, Peter Lyman, former university librarian at the University of California at Berkeley, commented, "We always talk about new technology using old vocabulary . . . . 'Electronic publishing,' 'digital library,' 'information highway': to our grandchildren these terms will probably sound as peculiar as 'horseless carriage.'"[2]

The occasion of Lyman's comment was a gathering at the New York Public Library in April 1996 of fifty distinguished library leaders from around the world. The general theme of the meeting was an effort to redefine the role of the library in the digital age. According to Lyman's quoted account of the meeting, there was a great deal of "linguistic fumbling" involved. This was likely due to trying to attach the discussion to a topic that had already moved beyond a language of collective comprehension. Ideas and issues can only be exchanged from mind to mind if the images conjured from the language of choice achieve some common understanding in the cognitive process.

There are new activities, initiatives, and dynamics in librarianship that are becoming recognizable, but they have not yet been named in a manner so they can be discussed on a broad, commonly understood basis. They are not yet a part of our library language. Defining these concepts may help us to understand the changing information environment that envelops our libraries, and may improve our steerage of them through a transformational passage into the information future. Examples of emerging themes to position in our language include distance information, managed information, and transformational budgeting.

Technical and Educational Background

A review of the transforming information and educational environments can help clarify the forces that are producing these powerful new themes. There are few areas of library effort that have escaped the tremblings of the information upheaval. These same instabilities have compressed time and distance, affecting their role in information access and delivery. These instabilities are also affecting the very foundations of the educational process.

Until information is needed it hardly matters where it resides. Geography is of little consequence except when it involves the delivery of library materials from traditional collections. The location of digital information servers is insignificant. If distance is not dead, it is certainly dying. Every hypertext location is immediately present to any other location, every document is a proximate one to the other, every visitor on the Web is in virtual assemblage. In cyberspace all roads lead to a digital Rome.

Time is still an important factor, but zones may set library clocks completely different from Greenwich Mean Time, solar time, and variegations based on arbitrary geographic boundaries and the seasons of the year. A colleague recently commented that projected revisions of college and university library standards were estimated for completion in about five years, but remarked that this was an estimate based on "ALA time."

An announcement reporting the likely release date of a software upgrade acknowledged that with the rapid changes in "Web time" it was becoming increasingly difficult to assert dates with certainty, or to determine when frequent upgrades to software would quickly leave applications and equipment obsolescent. Many systems and applications seem to stay in perpetual beta states these days, with production versions hardly in place before a willing world starts fretfully polishing a new revision.

The greatest danger of changes in the geometries of distance and time is the capability they possess to conflict with human comprehension and control. Nevertheless, the promises they hold are numerous, and the opportunities they present can already be felt not just in information systems but also in the timing and location of the educational process itself.

Educators are migrating from the notion that education should be teacher-centered towards a model in which the process is learner-centered. The integration of computing and telecommunication into this process potentially frees the school and scholar from the current restraints of place and distance, alters the influence of time, and encourages the integration of distance education into the learning process. In cyberspace any element of the scholarly process can be centric at any time, or at all points in place and time, whether it be the teacher, the student—or the library collection. That is, every element can be virtual except the socialization process. Social development, it should nevertheless be acknowledged, is not isolated to the educational institution during an individual's maturation. All of one's growing up is not done in school.

The employment of distance education may well shake apart the fundamental distinctions that have held for so long between the locations at which the teaching and learning processes have taken place, and may now dislocate the distinctions between the very institutions that have provided the educational experience itself. The trifocals of K–12, higher education, and continuing education may be transmuted into a lens that is a lineless, seamless, lifelong learning environment. Can we expect a more placeless role for the educational institution? Can we expect a more uniform continuum of education and learning throughout a person's life? Perhaps so.

Distance Information

Distance education provided in any guise must be supported by appropriate information sources. Libraries will continue to be the primary selection arbiters, organizers, and providers of information for scholarship. Libraries will increasingly rely on remote access as well as on the collections at hand to assist their users. They will rely on both local and distance information.

Distance information is meant to suggest remote access in the broadest of senses. Included in this definition are the application of interlibrary services in all its variations, document delivery in its many manifestations, and the creation and distribution of information objects from a multiplicity of sources. Distance information services are likely to be accompanied by new types of library-provided assistance. These may include regularly staffed, nationally distributed interactive help-desks; electronic messaging among librarians and other information professionals, teachers, learners, and mentors; the sharing among institutions of human expertise to provide specialized subject assistance; and the use of information know-bots and Web crawlers using every hour of the day to trawl out information to help the knowledge seeker. "Push services," like current-awareness services before them, are likely to come quickly.

Internet engineers and librarians are striving to mend the inchoate state of the Web. Plans incorporate the concepts of library cataloging and classification schemes into a refinement of the systems that sift the Internet for the most pertinent content relevant to an inquiry. Librarians have assumed a major role in the development and management of tools and content for this new information world. Improvement will be better achieved if everyone involved, librarians and others alike, share a confluent vision and vocabulary.

Despite a great deal of IT collaboration, far too many information technology professionals are still not fully aware of the importance of librarians to distance education. Distance information is a concept that requires broad discussion and understanding, if for no other reason than to secure the claim of libraries to their necessary role in the distance education process.

Managed Information

The inability of libraries and their funding parents to keep up with the continuing escalation of publishing and inflation, with the demands for both additional paper-based and digital information, and with the requirements for a powerful technical base and advanced human skills to control this information complex, has seen the introduction of completely new schemes for funding and managing the information environment.

Libraries have used cooperative networked arrangements for many years to construct bibliographic databases to effect cost savings and to share information, to help meet new service demands and circumvent financial strictures, and as a foundation for other resource-sharing efforts. But most cooperative arrangements in the past have been self-generated by librarians who have seen the wisdom of working together to solve problems—by working from the ground up.

As library funding bodies have determined that there is no way to meet the full costs of service demands and rising inflation rates, there has been increasing pressure and persuasion from them urging libraries to join in new kinds of consortial arrangements to leverage limited resources—financial, infrastructural, and human—and to provide mechanisms for productivity measurement and accountability. This results in information management from the top down.

To effectuate this approach, "information management organizations" are being established among libraries just as health-care management counterparts have been established in health services. This managed information approach attempts to build a common computer-based and telecommunications-supported infrastructure through which libraries can more easily share information, participate in consortial information purchases to reduce costs, and more centrally coordinate what has been a very decentralized system of collection building. This approach is also seen as having the virtue of extending the range and depth of information available to each of the participants.

Early in 1996, an article in the *Chronicle of Higher Education* observed that a growing number of institutions were establishing library consortia "to combine their purchasing power and win better deals" for access to electronic resources. "Statewide efforts already exist in Alabama, Georgia, Illinois, Louisiana, Ohio, Virginia, and Texas," the article notes, "while interstate groups have been formed among Big Ten research universities and among small liberal-arts colleges."[3]

This activity had become so widespread and vigorous that by the fall of 1996, *Library Hi Tech* had produced an important double issue that described in useful detail library resource-sharing programs in forty-six states.[4] Describing Web connectivity as a "fundamental empowerment technology," editor C. Edward Wall noted that it had become "an extremely high priority of state libraries, agencies, consortia, legislatures, and offices of the governor—across the United States" in expanding access to information resources.

Most of the organizations that have been shaped across the country seem quite similar to the general model of a top-down rather than a bottom-up organization. Libraries appear to have the option to participate or not in these evolving managed information organizations. But it is obviously difficult for an institution to choose not to move its regular funding and cooperative energy towards commonly agreed to, shared programs if it wishes to benefit from information-management seed funding and the other benefits to be gained from consortially scaled partnering.

Information vendors like this consortial approach very much. It assures a market; it pretty much guarantees a high level of regularized transactions or licensing income; and it is likely that business transactions will be handled centrally through a representative of the information management organization, not through the individual selectors or purchasing agents of every participant.

Inherent in such approaches, however, is the fact that libraries inevitably will give up some degree of local choice. There is also the danger that every participant will be dragged to some mid-level common denominator. The quality of present centers of scholarly excellence may be reduced, unexpectedly promoting the leavening of research resources for haves and have-nots alike. Every library should have the opportunity to lift itself—and help others lift themselves—to the highest level of technical, collection, access, and service capability possible. Sustaining great libraries should not diminish other libraries. It adds to, builds up, and enlarges the capabilities of other libraries, and such institutions are themselves strengthened in turn through their collaborative association with others.

There should also be concern that a concentration of information management at a state level, at a university system level, or at whatever level an information management organization functions below the present national cooperative level, may well represent a threat to those networked cooperative programs that have served libraries so well the past twenty-five years. Federating new library cooperative programs could well break apart the present national, networked structure. Rebuilding a national bibliographic wheel on a state-by-state basis would be absolute idiocy. Whether collecting and information-sharing cooperatives can be established that will not harm the national cataloging metadata structure remains to be seen.

Managed information practices are finding an active place in the contemporary library scene. The concept needs to be incorporated into the library language so that discussions of the serious issues involved can proceed more easily, with a fuller understanding of how present resource-sharing practices are evolving from those of the past.

Transformational Budgeting

The development of information management organizations reflects yet another instrument for change that could evolve in the administration of libraries. This provides for the allocation of fiscal and other resources on a different basis than is traditionally the case. This concept is defined in the phrase "transformational budgeting."

The capability of institutions, and especially of educational systems or funding authorities overseeing a group of libraries, to influence the directions that libraries will take given the persuasive power of funding is not surprising. The budget process can be used to move libraries through transformational processes they might not otherwise be capable of—or care to experience.

There has been a great deal of joking about the difficulty in moving university faculty or officers toward a common goal, like herding cats, they say. There is at least one thing that will herd anything: money. This became abundantly clear during the early days of the Higher Education Act's Title II-C grants, when libraries quickly engaged in cooperative or targeted activities in order to grasp the new funding opportunities directed at strengthening research libraries. This is likely to repeat itself, as agencies look to the use of pooled rather than individually distributed funds to support libraries. Federal funds are being directed toward larger-scale digital library initiatives, and telecommunication deregulation dividends are providing more support for the technical infrastructures of schools, hospitals, and libraries. Funding from the National Digital Library Project at the Library of Congress is driving libraries toward major digitization efforts more quickly than might otherwise be the case.

Economics is encouraging cooperative activity at several levels. Libraries should anticipate experiencing more examples of the application of transformational budgeting at state and system levels. The establishment of managed information organizations and targeted funding, as previously described, will surely be joined by additional similar measures. It is certainly in the best interests of libraries themselves, and of organizations of every sort, to accept (thoughtfully) and use (carefully) the concept of transformational budgeting to help ease the way through the major changes that all are experiencing at such a rapid rate—a rate in which the clocks of change appear to have gone mad.

Transformational budgeting can influence library activity from the top down, but it can also be applied very powerfully at the local institutional level within the library itself. Common sense suggests that every library manager should attempt to direct every possible dollar, every extra dollar added to the library budget toward the solution of problems, not simply toward maintaining the status quo or trying to recapture the lost ground of traditional collections, canceled subscriptions, or downsized staff.

Transformational budgeting should incorporate the dedication of funds for the development and training of staff, and for better informing and educating library users and administrators regarding the issues that confront libraries today. It should support the enhancement of the computing and telecommunication infrastructure that is required to extend traditional collections through distance information. It should help make personal access to network computers as ubiquitous as possible. Local resources should also be directed toward appropriate institutional participation in managed information organizations and in trans-institutional, even global, partnerships—in substantial digitization projects, for example; in sharing collections; in shared collection development itself; and in sharing digital information and human expertise.

Many types of resources can be budgeted towards transformation. An attempt should be made to leverage every library dollar, leverage every hour of human labor, use every hour of Greenwich or Web-time available, reward every significant staff achievement, and stimulate every creative idea towards progress and quality. Transformational budgeting should be a major strategy incorporated into the tools that library managers can use to address the problems that have seemed so insolvable over the past dozen years.

Themes, Concepts

Transformational budgeting, distance information, and managed information are themes to include in a new conceptual library vocabulary. They can help libraries understand the changes they face and provide a context within which they can effect the ongoing improvement of their management, their programs, and their services—while also understanding what may be lost in the process of change.

Understanding something does not necessarily make it good. There are a number of risks for libraries in pursuing the practices that lie behind each of these themes. Defining them, however, makes each more accessible to a reasoned understanding, and may enable us to better appreciate what these practices can help us accomplish. Such definition may also make clearer the possible negative consequences they may hold which libraries had best keep in cautionary mind.

Change is difficult. Many persons are convinced that moving into a new paradigm will result in leaving an Eden behind. The contours of the information future are not clear. By nature, librarians require a feeling of control and closure, and the information future today feels as unappreciable as cyberspace itself, much like St. Bonaventure's view of the Absolute: "an intelligible sphere, whose center is everywhere, whose circumference is nowhere."

Ideas have long shadows. Those shadows may not last unless the language that defines them is refreshed for a new era. Ideas may have no more impact than shadows if they are not fleshed out through definition and action. Can we discuss the library issues of today in the more limited language of libraries twenty-five years ago? It is unlikely, and we had better move on with defining fresh conceits in the information present if we are to deal with the issues of tomorrow.

NOTES

1. Harold Billings, "Magic and Hypersystems: A New Orderliness for Libraries," *Library Journal* 115 (April 1, 1990): 46–52. (See also chapter 2 in this book.)
2. Peter Lyman, as quoted in William Grimes, "Libraries Ponder Role in the Digital Age," *New York Times,* April 29, 1996, B1.
3. Thomas J. DeLoughry, "Purchasing Power: Cost-Sharing Efforts Help College Libraries Finance Electronic Acquisitions," *Chronicle of Higher Education* (February 9, 1996): A21–22.
4. "State of the State Reports: Statewide Library Automation, Connectivity, and Resource Sharing Initiatives," *Library Hi Tech* 144 (1996). A useful discussion of five statewide information-sharing consortia can be found in William Gray Potter, "Recent Trends in Statewide Academic Consortia," *Library Trends* 45 (winter 1997): 416–34.

10

~~~

Special Collections
Still Special after All These Years

To answer the question posed of why special collections are so special, it is interesting to consider whether such collections are still as special as one might have believed they were in the past. The question particularly intrigues me, since I was asked to present a paper in November 1976, as part of the University of Texas at Austin's Graduate School of Library Science Colloquium Series, to wit—"What's So Special about Special Collections?" Has my view or have circumstances changed during that time?

My perspective then was that of a university administrator with line responsibility for one of the great Latin American collections in the world, for the most comprehensive collection of Texas-related materials in existence, for very young area collections of Asian and Middle East materials, and for a two-year-old Mexican American Library Program. Moreover, I had recently been made chief collection development officer of the university library, and was helping organize and process the vast collection of rare and special materials that was forming the Harry Ransom Humanities Research Center. These responsibilities had been whetted by personal scholarly and bibliographic pursuits among those collections.

Returning to that paper a quarter of a century later, from a perspective undoubtedly changed by time, I continue to find a great deal

This article was originally published in *RBM: A Journal of Rare Books, Manuscripts, and Cultural Heritage* 1, no. 1 (2000).

of resonance in the ideas expressed earlier. The word "special" can be applied to a variety of collections, but there are several constants that most such collections share with others, or that distinguish them from others. Special collections can be distinguished by subject content or language and area of the world, by format, by level of rarity, by sheer expensiveness, or by the special research value that the comprehensiveness of associated materials brings.

Special collections still share in the distinctiveness of the higher level of costs they entail. The general expensiveness of their contents, the difficulties of their acquisition, the need for staff with special skills to select, acquire, process, and service them are all elements that contribute to higher costs than those for a more general library. Additional expenses include special requirements for housing, preservation and conservation, and security. These issues are as true today as they were twenty-five years ago, just as there will always be a need for collection development policies and aggressive acquisition programs for them, for publicizing and promoting a wider use of those materials that pride of ownership might otherwise discourage.

Exhibits, special catalogs, and the routine publication of information about the holdings of a special collection were encouraged in that 1976 paper. The assertion that "Materials must be used, not sealed from use" is as applicable today as it was then. A careful balance between service and preservation continues to be a special concern for special collections.

That earlier paper suggested, "It is increasingly important that institutions share their resources with others" and acknowledged, "The use of machine-based cataloging and indexing systems is going to be an increasing element in accessing special materials." The dimensions of the technological advances that would someday apply to special collections, whether they were used to create digitally encoded finding aids to make holdings more widely known, or to digitize materials themselves as a means of sharing them, could not have been readily imagined.

I suggested the now-primitive usefulness of making special collections more easily available to undergraduate students "by making videotapes . . . which could be shown on the Closed Circuit Television monitors in the Undergraduate Library." Digital exhibits of the treasures held by our libraries have certainly leapt far beyond that notion. A new means of delivering music, video, and other media via the Internet probably will seem primitive in the near future.

Perhaps more than the building of any collection, the development of special collections still represents a singular investment in "anticipation of use." This acquisition principle may suggest investments in objects representative of intellectual, artistic, and emotive values that may outweigh their more immediate benefit to the processes of research, learning, and even the preservation of culture. Who knows when the work of a young artist or author collected today in anticipation of future growth and significance and study will be proven right or wrong?

Extra effort will always be needed to convince funding authorities that the building of special collections is just as important as the acquisition of current publications—the infrequent use of much of which we generally remain too embarrassed to admit. It is clear that unless special collections are continually enriched, they will become museums bereft of the life that encourages learning and fresh research.

One special concern about such collections pertains today just as it did in the past. That is the need to identify the role that a special collection holds within the institution. How does it relate to the institution's mission and that of its general library collections?

It was cautioned in that 1976 paper that "parochialism, provincialism, elitism are easy traps" for the staff of special collections, with the danger of their being "left behind" by the professional progress of staff engaged in broader library activities. Hindsight suggests that the compartmentalization of staff can be just as serious from the other point of view. Staff involved in traditional collections and services should be aware of and understand what their colleagues are about in special collections, branch libraries, and even different functional divisions or departments, as every group should be.

The similarities are clear, and changes are apparent between these scenes separated by a quarter century. Financial constraints have somewhat slowed the purchase of rare book collections for academic libraries over that period. But time continues to construct rarities as materials sit in the stacks—or in databases. The growth of area studies collections is probably still not proceeding at the anticipated level, and new formats and interests now command attention beyond many targets of the past.

A number of funding opportunities and special projects have led to much greater bibliographic control of library holdings in general, but new digital applications, standards, and the language of the Web will soon enable even broader and deeper access than is now the rule. Copyright and intellectual property issues have achieved a level of concern that far transcends that of just a few years ago. When all is said and done, however, there should be no question that an appropriate balance will have been achieved that recognizes the rights of the creator and the rights of scholars.

The national waves that have swept across libraries over the past twenty-five years—shared collection building, bibliographic control, preservation and conservation, resource sharing—are being joined by the sweep of digitization. The ongoing unification of these elements of information management will continue to make our libraries more accessible, less constrained by time and distance. A fuller distribution of information about special collection holdings, and the availability of digital representations of the original work, will increase in years to come.

Special collections will be shared more readily via digital delivery, on-site surrogates, and combinations of media yet to be created. The special expertise of library staff will be shared more broadly, probably online. Competition among libraries, uncurbed by rampant cooperation, will continue as keenly as it always has.

Special collections will remain as special in the future—after the waves of change, dearth, and conflict, after all this new technology and technology to come—as they always have, after all these years.

11

Shared Collection Building
Constructing the Twenty-First-Century Relational Research Library

The sea, the sea, is always rebuilding.
—Paul Valéry

Research libraries have always been constructed and reconstructed within the scholarly, social, and economic tensions of their particular place in time. Inexorably and irretrievably, our great research libraries in this, our time, are becoming part of an even greater whole: a massive relational library of traditional collections, digital libraries, commercial services, multimedia flow, and linked information resources of every kind that can respond to the particularized interests of the individual information seeker on a global basis. Our local institutions, our national library organizations, and this evolving global information structure must be built and rebuilt within these changing tensions to satisfy this very simple thing: serving the present and future information needs of individuals.

Libraries have been constructed by or for the individual user. Research libraries are built and rebuilt by institutions to serve each user. Increasingly, libraries are sharing resources of every sort—collections, digital information, human expertise—in order to meet this mission. And they are moving quickly beyond the physical site and time-bound collections of the past, taking advantage of new models of

This article was originally published in *Journal of Library Administration* 31, no. 2 (2000).

access and delivery to provide more—and more pertinent—information services.

The same environment that is facilitating an expansion of resource sharing among libraries also offers an opportunity for information partnering never available before, on such a collective basis, among entities that have not collaborated in quite the same way in the past. Libraries, authors, publishers, vendors, and information users require one another, and should leverage their resources to gain the most from this new environment.

More formal collaborative collection building among these entities seems desirable as this informational sea continues to swell whether we wish it so or no, and as information consumers rush to dip from it. The massive, twenty-first-century relational tool that is growing through the present haphazard collection-building of many information contributors can become a remarkable digital research library. More thoughtful collaboration in its construction, and the establishment of discovery devices to wrest what is most useful from it, will be required. A convergence of public, private, governmental, and individual efforts, for profit and not-for-profit, to shape this great relational library will profit our learning selves and those learners to come.

The Relational Library

Libraries have been relational in the fashion of their day. The importance of library collections lies in their ability to provide the resources that relate to a user's needs and interests. Pertinence is what matters. And information must be related to information, not only in content but also by connection. Do you recall Marvin Minsky's oft-quoted question: "Can you imagine that they used to have libraries where the books didn't talk to each other?" Books have spoken to books in the past when they have been read and connected through a common reader. The application of new knowledge organizational systems will eventually allow the linkage of text in books with content elsewhere in the networked information commons. Ideas will foment within or beyond walls even more heatedly than ever. For all their reputed quietness, libraries are loud with the communication between books and reader, of content with content, and the consequent busy construction of new ideas.

Librarians and library tools have provided the mediation that helped connect the reader with the content available in library collections—scattered ideas just waiting their assemblage to feed a mind or add a mite to the warehouses of knowledge. In the past, the establishment and maintenance of relationships were a function of the card catalog, indexes, finding aids, and human memory. That was the relational library in its traditional form.

Today, the digital library environment is improving the means by which information seekers can identify and retrieve the content most useful to them. In many cases, the new technologies enable tools that will routinely scout out ideas, an experience, a work of art, or some other construct for a networked user and deliver a personalized package of relevant content directly to that individual.

The information seascape can be scanned and relational linkages can help locate and deliver whatever is most relevant to the user's needs. This relational construct, this relational research library, will increasingly include content of every kind connected by the hooks and tags of applied metadata. The devising of new means for linking will shape the next generation of knowledge systems. The present Google-type search engine suggests a model from which a killer engine to search the entire contents of the knowledge cosmos will emerge.

Imagine a search engine with access to the total content of the Web, the WorldCat of the OCLC, the growing digital collections of the Library of Congress, the daily physical and digital gatherings of our research libraries and small regional archives, the e-books and e-journal content available from commercial information distributors. Imagine an engine that can retrieve and connect this content and shape it to fit a knowledge seeker's needs. That engine is certainly under development in someone's mind, a laboratory, a garage right now. The human knowledge and imagination fields from which this engine can harvest will continue to be constructed from some of the sources described in this paper, but more cooperative and orderly collection building could make that very possible dream a more effective and practical reality.

The development of a global relational research library should become a major cooperative goal of libraries and their many partners in coming years. As this activity is pursued, a better understanding of the "spaces" within which such development and service will take place will be required: private spaces, public spaces, physical spaces, digital spaces—all of which house data, information, knowledge, libraries. It is almost the library as universe, the universe as library, of which Jorge Luis Borges dreamed—a metaphor for a mix of ordination and chaos, a labyrinth that Borges would surely recognize today as a space in which libraries seek order.

Personal Space Libraries

Technology already enables the Internet user to select linkages and content of all kinds, and to gather these into clusters of personalized data behind an icon on the computer display screen. These sites are frequently identified as "My Home Page," or "My Campus," or "My News," or my-this or my-that. The new technologies are also stimulating the construction of personal space libraries—"mylibraries," they might be called. These are collections of related ideational or data objects, gathered on an individual's personal computer, or in some other available private digital space, built to satisfy the scholarly or private interests of that person. This is true whether for the short term, in answering an immediate query; or for the longer term, in maintaining a group of selected sources at a personal website for prospective future use.

Nancy London of the OCLC, speaking at the "Online World Conference" in Chicago in October 1999, very aptly defined such a model as "an end user library within the library environment at large."[1] The library environment writ large includes a wide variety of spaces within which the results of collection building are housed.

In an important paper, "The Cultural Legacy of the 'Modern Library' for the Future," Francis Miksa of the University of Texas at Austin raises several interesting questions regarding library spaces that might well be contained within London's "library environment at large."[2] Miksa asks whether a return to the "private space" library of the past may be under way. And if so, what will be the effect on our large public space libraries?

Miksa suggests that the great personal libraries of the past gave way to the giant modern library—the "public space" library of the present—as the volume of publishing outpaced the ability of the individual's personal library to keep stride. The advent of the computer has made it possible, he suggests, for individuals to again build "private space" libraries within the vast realms of computer memory and the Internet, where there is room to spare. This will enable libraries, he says, "to shape such collections and their access mechanisms precisely for the needs of the individual or the cohesive group of individuals who require them."

The MyLibrary service of the North Carolina State University (NCSU) Libraries is an excellent example of how an academic library can make this type of personalized feature available to the campus scholar.[3] Its website points out that MyLibrary "integrates principles of librarianship (collection, organization, dissemination, and evaluation) with globally networked computing resources creating a dynamic, customer-driven front-end to any library's set of materials." The result is a customizable HTML page where "local and remote sets of data, information, and knowledge" are gathered for the scholar.[4]

Any campus library user may create an account on the NCSU system, select an area of primary academic interest, and customize the prospective MyLibrary contents from a choice of hotlinks. This system is distinguished by the multiple paths along which content can be sought by the user, or delivered to the user, based on the customized design of MyLibrary—augmented by "reactive/human mediated interactive assistance" from designated reference librarians and collection managers. The choice of personal links, quick searches, current awareness, and interactive personal assistance services represent elements of a highly personalized, relational research library tool.

Work on a knowledge system at the University of California at Santa Barbara also shows promise of elevating this type of customized collection building and retrieval to rather remarkable levels. The Alexandria Digital Earth Prototype project (ADEPT) will enable faculty members working in the field of geography to create digital library collections tailored to their teaching and research requirements. This ambitious project looks far beyond the present capabilities of the MyLibrary approach towards a new knowledge system.[5]

An ADEPT program will reach out across the body of geographical information as it exists in digital form—data sets, textual materials, aerial photographs, and computer simulation models—and assemble these into "information landscapes" that will help an investigator solve specific problems. "Iscapes," the project calls such assemblages of content and software, gathered from digital libraries and information servers around the globe. Software to provide specialized access and interface for the program is under development at the California Digital Library.

It is anticipated that individual personalized libraries can be constructed on demand to develop answers to what the project calls an "iscape query." The project will rely principally on the Alexandria Digital Library at Santa Barbara, "a digital collection now approaching 1.5 terabytes' worth of digital maps, remote-sensing images, and aerial photographs of the State of California."[6] The experimentation with iscapes in geography courses will be followed by introducing the iscape concept into courses in anthropology, biology, research studies, arts, and humanities.

Among the most interesting commercially driven, relational information developments presently under way is the CrossRef reference-linking consortium.[7] This nonprofit organization of over ninety major scholarly publishers is linking Web-based electronic journals and other Web-based content by means of the Digital Object Identifier (DOI) standard.

GraceAnne DeCandido has provided an instructive definition of the DOI in a paper for the Public Library Association: "The DOI is a unique persistent identifier of intellectual property in the digital environment."[8] Because the DOI is "persistent" (remaining with a digital information object throughout that object's lifetime), it is possible for publishers to mark a particular digital object—book, article, map, image—so that it can be linked across a body of digital literature or its access controlled or managed by its owner.

A scholar browsing an article in a journal that cites an article in another journal is able to link immediately from one to the other text if they have been marked with a DOI. A powerful relational tool can utilize the DOI to correlate the intellectual content of a work with its digital and physical manifestations. "CrossRef aims to become nothing less than the complete reference-linking backbone for all scholarly literature available in electronic form," Amy Brand, a spokesperson for the program, asserts. CrossRef expects to add encyclopedias, textbooks, conference proceedings, and other relevant literature to the nearly 6,000 journals currently included in the project.[9]

By utilizing these new linking systems, the digital research library of the future can be designed according to the demands of the user, its shape shifting as the user requires. But a great deal of content remains to be converted from its physical representation into digital format, even as many publishing sectors create new information in digital form. It is important to recognize that commercial Web-based vendors, like libraries and other nonprofit agencies, are adding massive amounts of content to the surging cybersea, as well as seeking additional means to link the information objects that reside there.

Commercial Web-Based Relational Services

Information e-commerce vendors on the Web are providing services that some have suggested represent a fuller range of relational services than libraries presently provide. Commercial entities frequently and obligingly supply Web customers with personalized, protean "my space" digital services. For a fee, or to encourage e-commerce, the Web is scanned by a vendor according to a profile established for the individual. A constantly rebuilding "my space" is then provided to the customer by the vendor, who reaps additional commercial benefit as the rebuilding continues. Baseball games are updated inning-by-inning, or play-by-play, on the Web. A click on "Reload" delivers fresh content just as quickly as news or text or media is modified. Advertising is rebuilt just as quickly. Commercial messages are redisplayed to a prospective customer with every update of the site, with routinely rebuilding banner ads, and through streaming entreaties to the customer to try out a new service.

Amazon.com has been cited as an e-commerce model that libraries should emulate to improve their services. A modest current awareness tool only, Amazon.com gives the appearance of being more personalized and extensive than in fact it is. Amazon.com is basically an object-distributing business, and is good at what it does. But it is not an information service—except as a purveyor of simplistic publishing, bibliographic, and purchasing data, and as the provider of several interesting relational services based on buyers' habits as revealed through implanted "cookies" on their computers.

These relational Amazon.com services suggest the prospective useful linking of scholars based on their common interest in a topic, or their use of a common informational site, in the global relational research library.

Another e-commercial area of service provides a different example of how libraries can extend their relational responses to the user. This service lies in the field of family history. Two of the most popular, successful, and innovative commercial services in the family history field are Ancestry.com and Genealogy.com. These services have constructed extensive digital data banks quite rapidly thanks to the volunteer and commercial energy that is converting both print and nonprint records into digital format and loading them into storage. Imagine all the genealogists in the world pouring their family history records into the Internet. These services already gather, store, relate, and deliver content of all sorts at an astonishing volume.

An inquiry regarding a distant family member, for example, can produce a page-set of pertinent data from a number of sources. These may include data available at Internet family sites, in articles listed in a "periodical source index," and from other commercial family history Internet-based locations. These services also include family message boards for chatting or posting inquiries and a formidable list of additional Web-accessible or printed tools. Relevant sources such as census records, cemetery records, court records, military records, immigration records, ship lists, vital statistics, maps, and similar sources are included. Increasingly, the full-text content is displayed, including digital images of the original documents. The assembly of this information on a single website, linked to dozens of other sites only a click away, is made possible by the metadata that collocates the content of this relational tool. A great deal of local history may need to be rewritten based on new facts that are coming to light through this process. The ripeness of data available from many sources and the linking capabilities available to the user permit the assembly of a family tree, a knowledge tree, as human ingenuity chooses.

Commercial websites can be modified, and styles and features changed, much more easily than can the full informational expanse of research libraries. But it is the case that research libraries—in their digital aspects—are assuming many of the characteristics of the type of commercial relational services described above. The use of metadata systems such as the Digital Object Identifiers standard is potentially applicable to any information-bearing object that exists or is represented in cyberspace.

Over time, research libraries will increasingly become more relational throughout their full intelligence scope, given the nature of the technological, social, and fiscal pressures that are generating change, and given the rapidly evolving relational technology. It will certainly benefit the library user or knowledge seeker if there can be a swifter construction of relational research libraries and a more rapid deposit of digital content into the information commons. The Internet already offers a vast bazaar of the best and the worst products and services that modern culture has to offer. It can become much more.

Shared Construction of the Relational Research Library

If the resource-sharing spirit of past years can be incorporated more deeply into contemporary shared-selection practices, adding new partners in the process, libraries can be constructed to satisfy a patron's particularized needs on a more distributed and extended basis. Shared collection building can be a mechanism whereby traditional collections and the newer digital content services—including commercial collections and services—can join in expanding this emerging relational library, an internationally linked "mother" research library of the twenty-first century.

An accretive process is already building this entity whether we intentionally plan to do so or not. It is building at this very moment, albeit rather willy-nilly, as digital additions from thousands of sources pour into the rich, rebuilding digital sea.

David Seuss of Northern Light once asserted that his firm was probably manipulating the largest body of knowledge in the history of the world.[10] In addition to what it is able to supply via the Web, Northern Light provides a pay-per-document service based on its holdings of over 25 million individual full-text documents in a Special Collections program it offers—another ancillary source of digitally provided information.

The opening of the Internet Archive in October 2001, with 10 billion web pages dating back to 1996, represents an enormous addition to the Web, but how these snapshots of web pages through several generations of change will contribute to scholarship remains to be seen. The physical contents of our research libraries, in fact, continue to constitute a far, far greater amount of scholarly substance than that presently available on the Web.

The quality of this rapidly growing Web-based library will improve as our libraries, commercial firms, scientific bodies, government agencies, volunteer organizations, and individuals contribute higher quality, standards-based, value-added information to it. Library information-management organizations have been building collections through collaborative selection and consortial purchasing of library materials and electronic services for some time. A number of cooperative models exist through which libraries collaborate to enrich the building and rebuilding of this information sea that is proximate to every intellectual shore. New content is being contributed through such programs as the Academic Image Exchange and the Making of America project, through numerous cooperative digitization projects, and through the encoding of local archival finding aids and the subsequent addition of archival content to the Web. The Library of Congress's American Memory program has been a successful model, helping stimulate many of these initiatives. In fact, the full extent of the LC's leadership in the establishment of digital library programs has never been adequately acknowledged.

JSTOR has proven how shared collection building can work successfully in developing digital access to retrospective journal contents. Project Muse has offered another model for providing access to current journal literature. The proffering of digital books offers a completely new venue for shared collection-building opportunities. EarthWeb's ITKnowledge service represented still another model whereby the constantly changing, constantly updated contents of some 5,000 physically published, key computer books were made digitally available on the database simultaneous-user model, but a market could not be developed rapidly enough to sustain such a narrowly niched business. Ebrary is introducing yet another model: look at a book for free, pay for download or print.

The Questia enterprise has been another aggressively constructed and promoted business vehicle for marketing e-book content directly to consumers rather than through a library or other middleman. However, its business plan never seemed viable, and it is likely that the warehouse of digital books that it has been building will be marketed by someone else in some other manner. Libraries should never have been concerned that Questia was going to usurp their role. In fact, any time an effective content-delivery system is created that will assist the information seeker, libraries should be the first to support such an extension or improvement of their own systems. Systems building on systems—hypersystems—provide the strongest means by which access can be magnified for the content seeker.

Electronic Book Sharing

The growing availability of electronic or digital books offers a different target of opportunity for libraries and publishers to cooperate in producing and providing access to these texts. (There are e-books and e-books. This chapter refers to an e-book service provided online through libraries, not e-books published to be sold directly to individual readers.) NetLibrary has been a good example of a business model for the successful distribution of digital books online, and especially for providing scholarly access to them. The contracts that netLibrary has established with reputable scholarly publishers, its arrangements with book jobbers to market its titles, a sensible business arrangement with libraries, and good technical features point towards a strong emerging model in e-commerce. Despite the financial problems that netLibrary has faced in maintaining market viability during the recent economic downturn in dot.coms and the information technology industry, it continues to offer the best example of how e-book commerce can thrive in a library setting. With its sale to the OCLC and the immediate resumption of its services, there should be every expectation that the size and scope of this venture will grow over time.

Either for an individual institution, or for a consortium of any size, there is the possibility for a vital service based on the netLibrary model. Libraries are going to have to consider carefully how such online services can be established to function on a cooperative collection-building or shared-selection basis in a consortial arrangement. A physical book and an electronic book live under different physical laws. A title available through the netLibrary e-book service can be delivered immediately, anywhere, at any time—unless another library patron is browsing the title or has it checked out for a longer period of time. Access to the title and its contents can be established immediately from an entry for the title in the online public access catalog or other digital finding aid.

Selections from e-books can be downloaded or printed quickly under standard fair-use policies. Reshelving the title is instantaneous, and maintenance, preservation, and security are such that a title should almost never be unavailable. Multiple copies can always be acquired to meet high demand. Titles available through these means will easily fit among the numerous other resources that are building in the digital information commons. And imagine! A book published in

Paris or Rio or Austin can be simultaneously available at locations around the world. Interlibrary borrowing of print-based objects could become increasingly a service of secondary resort, as it should be.

An International Digital Information Commons

Thus, in many places and programs, it is evident that a new sort of research library for the global community is being developed. That library is extensively relational in nature, constructed on a distributed basis by many participants, and takes advantage of the physical and digital objects that are being added to the global community's private, public, and commercial intelligence spaces. It should employ new economic models that leverage the financial resources of libraries and provide appropriate financial rewards for publishers and authors. Shared collection building, on a distributed, relational, and global basis, is becoming the model from which to construct the digital research library.

In an excellent paper on the ARL's Global Resources Program—whose principal stated goals are to improve access to international research resources, especially through cooperative structures and new technologies, and to help libraries contain costs—Deborah Jakubs comments: "We are already functioning in an interdependent system of access to information, but we have not yet called it by its true name, or developed it in a rational way."[11]

It should not be inferred from this discussion of linking information via digitally based connections that the physical collection has been forgotten. A major feature of this evolving information commons continues to be the growing physical library, with access to its holdings, and enhancements to those holdings, made possible through the linkages and relationships that information technology and knowledge systems are providing. For all that is available on the Internet, this store of superior content far exceeds that available in digital format. The challenge that should most excite librarians is the prospective melding of the physical and the digital, and the creation of a mechanism for fusing these modes of storage and delivery into the fuller bionic library that still lies ahead. This furthers that ongoing pollination of things art and things science towards a new flowering in humankind's reflections on the mind, our earth, and the universe.

A cross-pollination of the physical and digital in our library and Internet collections is the goal, and a shared construction of both will bring a more rapid genesis of the great information commons and relational library growing around us.

Several papers prepared for the Center for Research Libraries (CRL) conference, "Creating New Strategies for Cooperative Collection Development," held at Aberdeen Woods in Georgia in November 1999, include interesting suggestions for collection-building practices based on variations of "shared selection" or "cooperative" collection-development practices. There are many indications that international shared collection building is a concept rising in many minds. Neither governmental borders nor natural features of the geographical world should restrain cooperation and resource sharing from enlarging library collections or the digital information flow.

Anna H. Perrault, at the same CRL conference, provided several interesting suggestions concerning the need for collecting foreign printed publications on a cooperative international basis. She makes the point: "With the concept of an international information commons, there is the idea that whatever resources exist are available for the shared use of all. Is it possible that the Internet is engendering a mind set that makes the concept of an information commons more acceptable?"[12]

As an increasing portion of our research collections becomes a part of the evolving, digitally based relational research library, the more effective that global resource will be. Libraries can purposely help shape that commonly shared library's development. They must recognize the need for partnering among libraries, government, and the private sector—through the establishment of new forms of collaboration and resource sharing, through the application of metadata in a more organized fashion, and by the introduction of supportive global public policies. Learners can then find their way to a newly imagined universe of knowledge encompassing the globe.

"Over the years it has become almost a cliché to urge people to 'think globally, act locally,'" comment Milton Wolf and Marjorie Bloss in an Aberdeen paper. "Could we possibly add a parenthetical addendum to 'act locally (with global intent)'?" they ask.[13]

Peter Lyman of the University of California at Berkeley suggests that the opportunities that a global system offers have just not yet been recognized by the scholarly community: "At the turn of the twenty-first century, scholarly publishing is evolving into a global system of scholarly communication on the Web, including a spectacular array of multimedia texts based on visualization and real-time network communication . . . . It is striking that neither universities nor learned societies are prepared to sustain this work or to recognize it as a strategic opportunity to break the monopoly power of commercial publishers."[14]

A relational global library, building and rebuilding in a limitless digital sea, interoperable, constructed interdependently, offering customizably definable content to meet the learning and knowledge needs of individuals—that is what information cartographers are charting in this new century.

As Wolf and Bloss conclude: "After all, whether you realize it or not, we are building one library. And all of you are its bibliographers!" And so we are.

NOTES

1. Nancy London, quoted in *Advanced Technology/Libraries* 28 (December 1999): 10.
2. Francis Miksa, "The Cultural Legacy of the 'Modern Library' for the Future," *Journal of Education for Library and Information Science* 37 (spring 1996): 100–19. Available at http://www.gslis.utexas.edu/~miksa/modlib.html.
3. Available at http://my.lib.ncsu.edu/.
4. "MyLibrary: A Model for Implementing a User-Centered, Customizable Interface to a Library's Collection of Information Resources." Available at http://hegel.lib.ncsu.edu/development/mylibrary/.
5. Florence Olsen, "Researchers Seek to Build Data 'Landscapes' for Classroom and Lab," *Chronicle of Higher Education* (September 24, 1999): A39. The text of the proposal itself is available at http://www.alexandria.ucsb.edu/.
6. Olsen, "Researchers."
7. Calvin Reid, "STM Publishers Debut DOI Linking Service," *Publishers Weekly* 246, no. 46 (November 29, 1999): 24.
8. GraceAnne A. DeCandido, "DOI: The Persistence of Memory." Available at http://www.pla.org/publications/technotes/technotes_doi.html.
9. Amy Brand, "CrossRef Turns One," *D-Lib Magazine* 7, no. 5 (May 2001). Available at http://www.dlib.org/dlib/may01/05brand.html. "CrossRef Steps Up Pace of Linking Developments," press release, October 10, 2001. Available at http://www.crossref.org/press1010.htm. See also the International DOI Foundation website at http://www.doi.org/.

10. David Seuss, quoted in *Advanced Technology/Libraries* 28 (December 1999): 9.

11. Deborah Jakubs, "The AAU/ARL Global Resources Program: Both Macrocosm and Microcosm," *ARL* 206 (October 1999): 7.

12. Anna H. Perrault, "The Printed Book: Still in Need of CCD," a paper delivered at the Center for Research Libraries conference, "Creating New Strategies for Cooperative Collection Development," Aberdeen Woods, Georgia, November 1999. Available at http://wwwcrl.uchicago.edu/info/awccconf/awpapersgenl.htm.

13. Milton Wolf and Marjorie Bloss, "The Whole Is Greater than the Sum of Its Parts," a paper delivered at the Center for Research Libraries conference, "Creating New Strategies for Cooperative Collection Development," Aberdeen Woods, Georgia, November 1999. Available at http://wwwcrl.uchicago.edu/info/awccconf/awpapersgenl.htm.

14. Peter Lyman, "Knowledge Discovery in a Networked World," in *Information Alchemy: The Art and Science of Knowledge Management,* ed. Gerald Bernbom (San Francisco: Jossey-Bass, 2001), 51.

12

Giving Up Prophecy
The Future of Information Cooperation

Having recently had to review the progress of resource-sharing programs, information management organizations, library consortia, and their commercial cousins in which my institution participates, I am going to take off my usual evangelical robes and replace them with more cautionary ones. I know that these words from an old spiritual must surely be familiar as it asserts:

> *I ain't gonna study war no more*
> *I ain't gonna study war . . .*

Given sometimes to attempting too much prophecy, after looking over these programs and organizations I am going to quit forecasting. With the same strong certainty that those verses express, I am going to quit predicting anything—anything at all.

The information horizon that I have been observing for some time appears to have arrived. Information-sharing programs and information management organizations have marked a point of progress that is as far as I can see, and dimly through the fog at that. What lies beyond is impossible to discern.

This essay is a substantial revision of "TexShare and GALILEO: Comments on Managed Information Sharing," which was published in *Texas Library Journal* 73 (winter 1997).

The Rise of Cooperative Library Organizations

What *is* here on this event horizon? Just as the front edge of the infor-mation revolution as it related to libraries was marked by the Bibliographic Network Wars and the establishment by the library com-munity of various networks and other organizations in which to band together and confront change, so too at this point in the passage of change have several new groups been organized as redoubts from which to launch reactions and solutions. The history of library coop-eration in the United States is a long and complex one. The past activ-ities of consortia have been rich in resource-sharing success, in the common use of technical processing systems, in shared efforts dealing with "user services and everyday problems," in a focus on "special subject areas." The future of that type of activity is uncertain.[1]

The information revolution has led to new organizations that are more specifically directed at the transformational effects of the revo-lution, embodying efforts to manage knowledge, to manage scholarly communication, to redirect especially the science, technology, and medicine (STM) publishing massif. These organizations are active at several levels. At the macro level, there are the Scholarly Publishing and Academic Resources Coalition (SPARC) enterprise (gone inter-national), the Public Library of Science (PloS) initiative, and the International Coalition of Library Consortia (ICOLC) as the most easily visible. A new initiative, the Budapest Open Access Initiative (BOAI), is being initially underwritten and promoted by the Open Society Institute (OSI) and appears to be organized by the same prin-cipals behind SPARC and the PLoS. It is predicated on the principle that those works that "scholars give to the world without expectation of payment" should be freely accessible online.[2] However noble the idea, whether this effort grows legs remains to be seen.

It is not coincidental that these are all international initiatives. Since information acquired seven-league boots any location on the globe is now accessible with hardly a hop or a jump.

SPARC has brought mixed blessings. It has helped inform the aca-demic community about the many issues relating to scholarly commu-nication. It has encouraged the larger library community to consider how the scholarly publishing process might be reengineered. It has rather mistakenly promoted—at the expense of inter-information industry cooperation—the establishment of new, less expensive STM journals within a homegrown, academic publishing community as a means of displacing more expensive publications from long-standing major commercial publishers. It has rather aggressively attacked the commercial scholarly publishing industry through the "Create Change" and "Declare Independence" initiatives, encouraging retaliative, hostile statements from the publishing world—which is already guilty enough in some instances of damning libraries as pure contrarians. This has all helped fuel a very unproductive relationship between publishers and libraries.

Established without sufficient consideration of the consequences, the international Public Library of Science has attempted to persuade scholars to boycott journals that do not meet certain standards established by the PLoS. These standards are meant to force the establishment of a new model by which scholars will retain copyright and make journal literature "free" as quickly as possible. The PLoS plan was initially formed with a deadline of September 1, 2001, for the boycott, after which time authors pledged to submit articles only to publishers who had agreed to the PLoS standards. Thousands of scholars around the world signed onto the proposed boycott. The whole enterprise smacked of an inverse Cinderella story—massive commercial publishers would apparently turn from gilt carriages into pumpkins at the stroke of midnight on August 31, and bright, shining new publishing princes would appear with fully operable publishing infrastructures in place to distribute the scholarly word—for free. Nevertheless, the PLoS, like SPARC, has engaged the attention of the scholarly community with respect to the serious scholarly communication issues that affect libraries and academia. Once, it seemed that everyone just blamed libraries!

The International Coalition of Library Consortia has achieved a more positive dialogue among librarians, library network representatives, members of the information provider community, and other interested parties. ICOLC's "Statement of Current Perspective and Preferred Practices for the Selection and Purchase of Electronic Information" is an especially balanced set of recommendations that the scholarly community, libraries, and the publishing world— whether print or digital in orientation—could pursue toward more effective and equitable solutions that slight no one.[3]

Two other organizations are making significant contributions towards an effective technological and ideational base for a shared global library, and should not be overlooked as agents in helping manage information in better ways. The Coalition for Networked Information and the Digital Library Federation are each considered to be politically neutral and are each contributing to the establishment of standards and new ideas that will significantly enhance information linking and a shared global library presence. Nothing can be built that is stronger than ideas. Practical magic can never be as effective as cognitive magic. The strength of these organizations lies in their ideas.

Information-Sharing Opportunities

More easily identifiable to most libraries and more easily recognized as managed information efforts, at a more micro and practical daily level, are those organizations that focus on information sharing as a means to address the increasingly high cost and publication rate of journal literature. These are the OhioLINKs, the TexShares, the GALILEOs, the academic system and state-funded cooperatives. The similarities among these various resource-sharing programs are apparent. And there are far more similarities than there are differences among them. The major benefits of these resource-sharing organizations are obvious:

> They leverage resources through cost-sharing and consortial purchasing that produce major economies of scale.
>
> They utilize technology to remove distance and time as impediments to information access.
>
> They leverage human skills through a pooling of talent.
>
> They improve access to local collections and to that larger digital information commons building in the Web.
>
> They make distance information easier to provide in support of distance education and lifelong learning.
>
> They provide a mechanism by which information and learning can be extended on a more equitable basis to the full community of the knowledge needy.
>
> They provide a venue for the exchange of ideas and content, a forum for discussion and debate, and for an action-oriented body to inform and promote the interests of the group.

They may even create digital content or assume a role as publisher.

They accomplish these aims through the use of traditional and electronically enhanced interlibrary services; by the application of computing and new technologies that provide electronic access and digital library-based services; by the consortial purchase of e-books and full-text journals; by the encouragement of digitization projects; through easier scalability of programs and services; and through the unbelievable linkages that hypertext, metadata, and new coding enable.

There are, however, other similarities among these cooperatives that are of concern.

One issue is the fact that these organizations heavily represent—based on their funding and administrative direction—what I consider the application of "managed information" principles. This approach represents top-down, administratively directed resource-sharing programs. These are unlike the grassroots type of library cooperative that libraries helped build and have grown accustomed to over the past twenty-five years. Through these "managed" programs, a funding authority pretty well dictates the type and scope of resource sharing undertaken by members of the consortium. That authority may also wish to more tightly constrain and limit the potential "political action" component of the organization. There may simply be impediments because another administrative level is introduced, one that will most likely never quite understand the issues.

Library members of managed information organizations can certainly benefit from this directed participation. Their administrations rightly see that resource sharing is an effective means to leverage resources. But those same administrations—or legislators, or other funding authorities—may believe that resource sharing will resolve all the problems so widely visible these days in the flow of scholarly communication. Librarians know that is not the case.

Experience indicates that improved library access by electronic means tends to enhance the use of physical collections and increase dramatically the use of digital text collections, but comparatively little of the physical has been replaced by digital formats. Digital library usage and management appear to be more efficient than that of traditional collection programs. Access to content in electronic format can be extended to more users, improves the effectiveness of knowledge seekers, commands more use of all available and pertinent information, and reduces the rate of increase in the cost per information unit delivered to the user.

Managing the Costs

But digital access has not yet demonstrated that it can reduce the total infrastructional costs required to maintain currentness with the evolving technologies, to pay for life cycle maintenance of equipment and networks, or to manage the growth in publishing or other distribution of ideas that surge from the learning and knowledge enterprise. Costing out these models has never been done, but a start has been made. The "Statement" on electronic information developed by ICOLC provides guidelines that, if widely adopted, could help develop tools to measure useful management data towards improving the entire information flow.

NetLibrary has "commissioned and sponsored" a study of life cycle costs of library collections—the first phase focusing on the physical collections of research libraries, the next to study life cycle costs of electronic books. Initial results indicate that "the purchase price of acquiring a collection is a small fraction of the life cycle costs of maintaining it." Further, "The results demonstrate that monographs dominate the cost structure of a research library, consuming approximately 95 percent of library resources."[4]

It appears that the word "monographs" as used in this study refers to all the physical volumes in a library—"books and periodicals in a bound paper format." For comparative purposes, other physical formats (e.g., current serials, microforms, government documents) have been converted into book equivalent (BE) costs to enable an evaluation of the proportional cost impact of other formats on a total library budget. (It was estimated, for example, that the cost of a current serial subscription had a relative BE cost of 0.5 percent—a figure that most librarians will immediately mistrust.)

The report speculates that further study may support the contention that "costs associated with acquiring, accessing, and maintaining eBook collections may be less than the cost of maintaining hardcopy monograph collections." It is important that additional study include the combined complements of physical and digital content that comprise the modern library, and consider how additional reductions in costs might accrue through consortial and managed information approaches.

While such studies may prove useful in planning for the evolving library model, it is crucial that university and college administrators never believe that funding for specifically local academic library interests is no longer as necessary as it was in the past. By participating in consortia with specific financial demands routinely required to be paid, libraries may also be losing a level of independence, losing a level of local choice that is not possible in the larger group-shared selection process.

The Shared Collection-Building Model

This digital library activity is simply mimicking, to some degree, collection development programs that have long been part of the physical library model. It is apparent that libraries are moving, or attempting to move, toward blanket order programs (consortial acquisitions) for shared electronic services, for e-books, and for full-text journal files on a multiple, rather than single, institutional basis—just like cooperative blanket book orders. The activities pursued thus far have been based more on intuition than on research, historical documentation, and analysis of costs and benefits. Studies like that made by netLibrary (which initially seem rather self-serving) may help sharpen further comparisons between different programs. Research can help address those many questions posed by participation in information management organizations.

Is each library member of a consortial program going to have to help pay for sources and services that its users may hardly ever require? That appears to be the pattern, although the greater access may well be worth the (assumed) proportionally smaller cost of each information unit that is available through a consortial purchasing or leasing arrangement. Even the newest and smallest of libraries can gain, through consortial membership, access at any distance, at any time, for any purpose, to shared world-class library collections. Collections can be built, as it were, for small new institutions that would have taken many years and untold dollars to construct under former circumstances. An easier extension of knowledge and learning to the information-deprived and to the fuller citizenry may well result.

Many libraries asked at the time whether it made sense for Ohio's legislature to spend $21 million over a three-year period for electronic access to all of Elsevier's journals for forty libraries in the state of Ohio. It did not seem then that each library could benefit by access to those hundreds of scientific and technical titles—and that it would have been preferable to direct such a large sum in a manner that would better assist each library to gain access to information that would meet its specific needs. The economics of information distribution have changed, however, and in retrospect that choice makes good sense. These "big deals," as they have been critically characterized, are becoming more common since they can be very effective at extending access and reducing costs.

Furthermore, a collaborative planning process by the Yale University Library and Elsevier Science to create a digital archive for over a thousand journals published electronically by Elsevier could result in a major step toward a broader solution to the preservation of digital formats. This type of cooperative project represents a more positive direction for libraries to pursue with publishers than the arbitrary and contentious position taken by too many in both communities.

Ann Okerson, who is directly involved in Yale's participation with Elsevier in this archiving initiative, and who coordinates efforts by the Northeast Research Library Consortium to acquire online journals and services to the best advantage of the participants, has called for the development of shared solutions by everyone involved in scholarly communication: "If we collaborate and conspire together—researchers, publishers and librarians—we will discover again what we already more than suspect, that good will and common purpose can prevail around these tables, even the long-contested tables. Extremist language and extremist imagery are out of place and have an obstructionist effect. If we can set aside extremism, I believe we can already see around us the elements of new forms of publication that are inspiring and encouraging."[5]

There is, however, still another major issue. Are we lifting all boats in a more tightly directed use of resources? Or are we potentially reducing libraries to a lower common denominator because more resources are going into shared programs for the many, rather than more fully funding those centers of excellence from which the many can draw information riches that might not otherwise be assembled? This is a matter that requires careful, ongoing scrutiny.

A component of managed information sharing that must be devised is a means to customize hyperlinking so that systems meet the needs of individual institutions and scholars, so that choices can be reduced to meet the specific, carefully defined needs of any user. Again, a number of services based on the use of Digital Object Identifiers and open-record harvesting are being studied and established. The development of standards to be required in the digital publishing process is imperative to the coming federalism inherent in a global information commons—and to the successful retrieval of matter relevant to the searcher from that commons. "Reference linking" is a phrase and a process that will dominate library language in the future just as much as words like "resource sharing," "access," "preservation," "cooperative cataloging," and "information revolution" do today.

To Thy Funding Source Be True

State funding supports many of the cooperative programs that emerged during the 1990s. Investments of public monies now assist organizations like OhioLINK, Illinet Online, TexShare, VIVA (Virtual Library of Virginia), Georgia's GALILEO, and LOUIS (Louisiana Library Network). Given that most libraries, especially those in publicly funded academic institutions, have a first obligation to the cooperative program closest to home, there would appear to be little financial room available for additional participation in those many other regional, national, and privately established consortia whose programs increasingly resemble one another. What criteria determine the choice by a library of commercial brokers whose products and services may be available through several membership groups?

Since public money must go inevitably to participation in statewide consortia, public institutions will find it increasingly difficult to identify the resources to sustain an affiliation with programs of other organizations that require payment for their own membership and programmatic costs. Many libraries belong to university systems, or to institutions whose first calling must be to a local consortium. The potential conflicts for membership in other organizations are becoming more numerous. Participation with the many on a scale that is almost demanded today is time-consuming, resource-demanding, important, questionable, impossible to continue, impossible to leave.

Can the non-state, member-funded groups find sufficient grip and purpose to survive if additional state-supported cooperatives are established and pry their public-funded members away from the independent organizations? Ultimately, the availability of financial resources and the market will decide.

Libraries also appear to be running into themselves programmatically from several directions. Regardless of their fiscal obligations, or envisioned opportunities, or whatever else drives libraries into cooperative programs, this is the case. How many resource-sharing programs can an institution belong to when the programs consist only of interlibrary services and access to cost-shared, consortial electronic-information services? As Peggy Lee sang, "Is that all there is?"

Interdependence is developing among consortia members based on the need for each partner to maintain its participation in the shared programs—if reduced costs are to continue. This is a threat that cannot be ignored. It is important for all members that each member be able to pay its fair share of the (reduced) costs. Thus, there is increasingly a mutual interest in the annual improvement of each member's budget, sufficient unto meeting its partnership costs, so that full consortial benefits can be sustained throughout the group. It is ironic that libraries in the past did not have to be as concerned about the resources available to their colleagues as they are now.

A seat at the table may perhaps be worth the cost for participation in an organization. It is easier to critique programs and help direct them into more favorable seas and winds when one has paid for the privilege—although many times efforts to influence the direction of glacially entrenched library programs appear daunting. Cooperation does not suggest uniform agreement. It means working through various scenarios toward agreements based on dynamic consideration and discussion of alternatives. Librarians on occasion can be too lemming-like for their own good. The compulsive rush toward supporting a questionable program like the Public Library of Science is an example of the negative face of this reflex.

The author is reminded of his affection for the gorgeous style, the attention to the natural order, the prodigality of thought of Sir Thomas Browne, whose reflections grace several of these pages, but who remained convinced throughout his life that magic and witchcraft prevail in the natural world just as much as herbs, the networked rootage of trees, and the nag of human procreation. When a national organization (SPARC) sets out to resolve a cost-of-journal problem by urging the creation of yet another journal, a duplicate in topic at that, and distributes a build-it-yourself guide for establishing competitive new journals, the contradictions of sense and nonsense that afflicted Sir Thomas seem to have been replicated in the programs of this organization. A colleague observes, "Once we had one expensive journal on this topic to pay for. Now we have two." Membership in an organization like SPARC provides the legitimacy for positive criticism and an opportunity to suggest alternative schemes. In the longer term, one can hope the variety of fresh initiatives that such a powerful organization might mount will lead towards more effective transformations of scholarly communication.

Maintaining the Infrastructural Garden

Science is going to happen. Humanities scholarship and art are going to happen. Writing and reading are perennials. What continues to be singularly important in the scholarly communication process resides in the infrastructure, the connections within and between, where publishers, distributors, and libraries play their distinctive value-added roles. The historical partnerships of these players in the framework of scholarly communication must be retained. In devising a means by which the problems within the information flow can be resolved for the longer term, the continuation of the long path of this cooperation is more important than present managed information memberships. In the end, these are only fragile and transitory mechanisms waiting to be replaced by newer models.

As a conceiver of, a designer of, as a payer for, and as a strong believer in cooperative resource-sharing programs, I hesitate just a bit in sounding too loudly these cautionary notes. But I just don't see where these organizations are going beyond where they are at the moment. Or at least I am not going to forecast what will become of them and of those organizations with which I believe our cooperatives are going to compete.

I do know several things that the digital utilities at the heart of these enterprises require or should ensure.

They need *more content* and higher quality content.

They need to incorporate more *multimedia* content.

They need to incorporate *course content* to support the distance learning programs that are growing rapidly.

They need to incorporate *digital versions* of locally held treasures so that children and ordinary citizens can enjoy and learn from these objects that many libraries hold, but which are simply too distanced by geography or wealth from those many who might benefit from them.

A coordinated, *national digitization program* is required, much like the one for preservation that proved so successful in the recent past.

The information available on the Internet, regardless of how it got there, must be screened for quality, selected for permanent digital preservation and accessibility, cataloged and organized and tagged so that library users can make the best use of the best that's there, just as we want in our physical collections. The knowledge organization "killer app" to accomplish this is yet to be constructed. It may well occur purely through an accident of genius, as most stunning advances generally do.

Beyond Today's Horizon

So I just cannot forecast beyond today's horizon what may become of these managed information cousins across the country and around the globe. I do know that they represent the human and fiscal resource foundations for the creation of potentially wonderful learning systems that we simply cannot now imagine. I know that we must support them, question them, build and dismantle them, and ensure they serve us in our own distinctive missions like any other tool.

For they are tools, and libraries must make them do what library users require—not let them cause libraries to unknowingly lay waste the infrastructure that has so long sustained our physical collections and that holds so much promise for the digital. It is these tools and the pools of information from which they draw that encourage and permit the pursuit of human progress, that provide the stuff from which the arts and sciences are newly created, and that feed the advancement of knowledge.

I promised that I would quit forecasting. But in thinking about cooperation I am going to return to that old spiritual one more time:

I ain't gonna study war no more
I ain't gonna study war no more
Gonna join hands with ev'ryone
Gonna join hands with ev'ryone . . .

Good luck to every cooperative venture, but study them well, because librarians must join cooperative hands not only with other librarians, but also with scholars, publishers, and others along the knowledge stream to gain through the sharing of many what each cannot attain alone. As librarians always have, as they always must. Ev'ryone.

NOTES

1. Sharon L. Bostick, "The History and Development of Academic Library Consortia in the United States: An Overview," *Journal of Academic Librarianship* 27 (March 2001): 128–30.
2. Available at http://www.soros.org/openaccess/.
3. Available at http://www.library.yale.edu/consortia/statement.html.
4. Stephen R. Lawrence, Lynn Silipigni Connaway, and Keith H. Brigham, "Life Cycle Costs of Library Collections: Creation of Effective Performance and Cost Metrics for Library Resources," *College & Research Libraries* 62 (November 2001): 541–53.
5. Ann Okerson, "What Price 'Free'?" (September 2001). Available at http://www.nature.com/nature/debates/e-access/Articles/okerson.html.

INDEX

Harold Billings is director of General Libraries, the University of Texas at Austin, a position he has held since 1977. He has served on the boards of several major national library organizations and has participated in numerous other groups and activities concerned with resource sharing, networking, and preservation. An untiring book collector and reader, Billings is the author or editor of works dealing with contemporary literature and bibliography, as well as numerous articles about library cooperation and the electronic information revolution. He is the recipient of the 2002 Hugh C. Atkinson Memorial Award.

OT 72 x 356